Some Vegetable Sacrifice

Some Vegetable Sacrifice

R. Scott Yarbrough

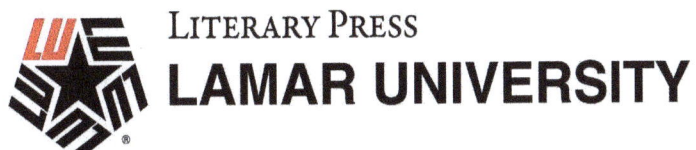

Copyright © 2020 R. Scott Yarbrough
All Rights Reserved

ISBN: 978-1-942956-73-0
Library of Congress Control Number: 2020943849

Manufactured in the United States

Photographs of Paintings:
Lori Cathey
Anna Boling
Robert Cope

Photo Editor of Paintings, Totem Pole:
Blaine Cathey

Lamar University Literary Press
Beaumont, Texas

For Sandi, York, Jenni (Chicken), Gloria and Rudy,
and Jason McMenamy

Other poetry from Lamar University Literary Press Includes

Bobby Aldridge, *An Affair of the Stilled Heart*
Michael Baldwin, *Lone Star Heart, Poems of a Life in Texas*
Charles Behlen, *Failing Heaven*
Alan Berecka, *With Our Baggage*
David Bowles, *Flower, Song, Dance: Aztec and Mayan Poetry*
Jerry Bradley, *Crownfeathers and Effigies*
Jerry Bradley and Ulf Kirchdorfer, editors, *The Great American Wise Ass Poetry Anthology*
Matthew Brennan, *One Life*
Julie Chappel, *Mad Habits of a Life*
Paul Christensen, *The Jack of Diamonds is a Hard Card to Play*
Christopher Carmona, Rob Johnson, and Chuck Taylor, editors, *The Beatest State in the Union*
Chip Dameron, *Waiting for an Etcher*
William Virgil Davis, *The Bones Poems*
Jeffrey DeLotto, *Voices Writ in Sand*
Chris Ellery, *Elder Tree*
Larry Griffin, *Cedar Plums*
Ken Hada, *Margaritas and Redfish*
Katherine Hoerth, *Goddess Wears Cowboy Boots*
Lynn Hoggard, *Motherland*
Godspower Oboido, *Wandering Feet on Pebbled Shores*
Gretchen Johnson, *A Trip Through Downer, Minnesota*
Ulf Kirchdorfer, *Chewing Green Leaves*
Laozi, *Daodejing*, tr. By David Breeden, Steven Schroeder, and Wally Swist
Janet McCann, *The Crone at the Casino*
Laurence Musgrove, *Local Bird*
Dave Oliphant, *The Pilgrimage, Selected Poems: 1962-2012*
Kornelijus Platelis, *Solitary Architectures*
Carol Coffee Reposa, *Underground Musicians*
Jan Seale, *The Parkinson Poems*
Steven Schroeder, *the moon, not the finger, pointing*
Glen Sorestad *Hazards of Eden*
W.K. Stratton, *Ranchero Ford/ Dying in Red Dirt Country*
Loretta Diane Walker, *Desert Light*
Wally Swist, *Invocation*
Jonas Zdanys (ed.), *Pushing the Envelope, Epistolary Poems*
Jonas Zdanys, *Red Stones*
Jonas Zdanys, *Three White Horses*
Jonas Zdanys, *The Angled Road*

For information on these and other Lamar University Literary Press books go to
https://www.lamar.edu/literary-press/

Acknowledgments

A book including images becomes a different universe. It is not a simple transference of words back and forth between artist and editor. The art has to be created, then, to make it look the best it can, I really needed photographers and photo editors on my end and then on Jerry Craven's end. I thank Lori Cathey, photographer, and Blaine Cathey, photo editor, who have generously shot numerous sessions in different lighting with different special needs. Due to the reflectivity of the fingernail polish, often we had to hold paintings in strange angles and try multiple lighting setups. One special shot for Blaine, in order to maintain a consistency in appearance, was shooting the Totem Pole—which in real life is twelve feet tall. It required that she get on top of the house, laying the pole on its back, and then shooting it in three sections, then later fitting the images back together to make it appear as one shot. Also, Robert Cope and the very talented Anna Boling for additional photography shots when Blaine, who now lives in New Orleans, and Lori who has to "work for a living"—both are nurses, one as an organizer of all the nurses in the Metroplex of Texas, the other as a transplant nurse in New Orleans. Anna even baby-sat the paintings in her trunk one weekend.

Another very strange difference in adding art is that I don't necessarily still own some of the pieces and therefore had to talk the owners into letting us shoot them or loan them back for a bit—a tedious process. Thus, thank you to Stephen Bennett and Dr. Elaine Schmidt. Special thanks to the frog I found during a run who gave his life for art. He was already run over; I did not do that.

Thanks also to many of my creative writing students, too, who freshly remind me of my journey to get to this point. Starlit Taie, Bridget-Scott Shupe, Mary Grace Biggs, Anna Boling (a talented writer as well as photographer), Michael Scott.

To the "Nail Polish Contribution Committee"—the many who have rattled through their hoards and cleaned out their nail-polish cabinets for me. I counted over twenty different shades (bottles) of blacks and grays alone used in "Rudy's Shoe." Amy Smith, Holly, and Heidi Hampton for their obsession with good nail polish who were especially generous donors. I counted over one-hundred-and-thirty bottles of polish donated.

To Jad Jabary who initially did a fair amount of input so I would not miss the first opportunity when Jerry Craven asked for me to send him some new work. Artists aren't always the best at logging and keeping up with their own work. My wife even joked that, "Wouldn't this have been so much easier if I were like Theo and just had put all your stuff under the bed."

To *Ink Brush Press* and reviewers of my last collection of poetry: Carol Coffee Reposa's review in the *Evansville Review*; Jerry Bradley in *Concho River Review*, and Diane Sahms-Guarnieri in *Fox Chase Review*. I am grateful to Dr. Peggy Brown, Dr. Dallie Clark, Darcy (the cat), Mike and Amy Fenning, Dr. Matt "Guitar" Coulter, Rachel Walker, Dr. Dean Kelly Andrews, Dr. Regina Hughes, Dr. Sean Geraghty, Tony Airhart, Dr. Kyle Wilkison, Ms. Weaver, and Deborah Hall.

Thanks to Darcy, a wonderful bit of sunshine in the neighborhood who avidly walked "Johnny Cash," her Australian Shepherd, every day and had befriended Erika in the "Squirrel" poem. She was the one who had noticed Ericka had been strangely absent and insisted we break into her house; we did and found her unconscious. After Erika was eventually in hospice in her own home, Darcy thought it a crime for her to be locked in her back bedroom to die. She moved her into the living room, changed her sheets from hospital white to plant prints, new pajamas, opened the windows, and let the squirrels continue their honest game with their dying nemesis.

Thanks to my family, immediate and extended. Many of these poems/paintings are a result of the avid storytelling obsession that comes from a golden childhood and family, from two parents who taught me what a truly functional family can be. I've never seen them fight; they love each other unconditionally. Thanks to my two brothers, Don and Steve, York and Kat and Jackson and Evie, Jenni, Sebastian, and Layla—kids, grandkids —and the Yarbrough/Davis Clan, who would all do anything for anyone in the family; to a wife I love as much as she loves ketchup, and to Peggy and Chris and Clif.

CONTENTS

11 Painting With Nail Polish
15 Floundering Lesson from an Oldest Brother in Matagorda Bay
17 Keith's Cancer
18 Jesus and Muhammad
20 At the Reservation: Sunrise Keeper
22 Dead Animal Game
24 Playing Bridge at the Nursing Home
25 Coyote and a Coupon
28 Ode to Carol Coffee Reposa's
    "Full—Stop" on Her Typewriter
        and Why I Prefer Pencils
30 Remember That Morning Just after Dawn?
32 Palate Man: Keeper of Right Turns
34 My First Southwest Flight
36 Ataxia
38 Upon Filling the Recycling Bin
41 Thanksgiving Poem
42 Chopping Cotton
45 Watching the KKK Rally in Sulfur Springs, Texas
46 What Does the Cuckoo Do Inside Her Clock?
48 Eulogy: Why Ericka Hated Squirrels
50 Bustie Girl and Charlie Pyewacket
52 Ignacho's House Burning Down
53 Notes from a Conversation: "How to Bet a Horse Race"
    According to Jim Jenkins [Live Stock Judge]
55 Makers of the Earth
56 David's Father
58 Bill Hall's Dog
60 Getting Old at Sam's Club
62 My Eye Exam from the Guy at Whole Foods
64 This One Round: Golfing Single
66 Mother and Beverly at the Alzheimer's Unit
68 The Best Lawn on this Side of the Block
69 Color
70 My Stupid Watch
72 Atlas in a Lawn Chair
74 Chores
77 Becky Watches Big Tex Burn Down
79 Going to the Dump in the City
81 Estate Sale
83 The Minotaur
95 Maiden's Name Game

Painting with Nail Polish

My best friend Rudy died shortly after Jerry Craven asked me to write a sort of "how I started using nail polish" for painting and "how the process developed." Rudy's wife Gloria waited a week to call to tell me and my wife. It was a tough call for her to make. She said, crying, "I'm not sure what to do with him."

I wasn't sure what to say—maybe that I as a portrait painter pictured him still in the arm chair with the remote in his hand and his Tabby in his lap, leaving me eternally waiting for him to change the channel, or perhaps he might be lying awkwardly in the lawn with the garden hose still and forever pushing a stream of water. While I stammered, looking for words, she added, "Oh, I had him cremated."

I suddenly understood her predicament: how do you say *goodbye* to ashes? Not only is he *just gone*, he's simply "not" anymore, as if he had become a *Bewitched* blink.

Flashback to years ago when I once visited my parents and noticed one of the first paintings I felt good enough about to display. It was a watercolor, my medium of choice. Mom had hung it proudly by the window, which is a death sentence for watercolor, though I did not know that at the time, nor did my mother. Over the years the sun drank back all the colors into its belly and left just a skeletal sketch, a dead animal, the bones of the finished painting. I begged her to allow me to repaint it, and she let me take it home.

It sat for several weeks until my wife, Sandi, who is good at motivation, said, "Go paint or clean the house." She was painting her fingernails.

I went in to get my watercolors in a cabinet where she also keeps her hoard of nail polish. I counted over seventy bottles. On a whim I multiplied seven times seventy to see how much money was in that cabinet. That was when the ideas came to me: fingernail polish doesn't fade; it is translucent, reflective; there are an infinite number of colors; each bottle has its own brush; it dries much like watercolor and fairly quickly. There had to be a brilliant brain of function in the heart of each tiny bottle.

So I stole what primary colors I thought she wouldn't miss and took them down to my poetry shack where I write and started to paint. The colors were amazing, like the real world captured in tiny bottles. I suddenly realized how many different blacks there *really* are, and how many oranges there are in a living orange, that even a piece of splintered wood holds a wheel of colors.

I also found out what "huffing" was when I tried to stand up three hours later. Rule one, always paint with nail polish in a ventilated room.

After that day I began looking at women's fingernails, often asking what color and brand they used—Opi and Essie are the best, though I'm kind of embarrassed to know that. I also discovered that women, for the most part, think it's thoughtful of me to notice their nails and even more so that I ask the brand and color.

I asked my wife, "Do you think there are women at your work who might want to get rid of some excess nail polish?" She insisted many would share their bottles because that would allow them to buy new polish; I would be their hero. It was thus that I found my "dealer" when, that Friday, she came home with a sack bulging with over two hundred polishes, from glitter to thinners, from "Just Before Dawn" to "Midnight," from "Sensual Sunflower" to "John Deere Green."

I experimented with different types of paper to see if that mattered; it did. Texture became part of the machine. Also, I discovered I could "push" the color/colors around as they dried, mixing them on the painting itself, sometimes with a stick or a toothpick, and once I used a ballpoint pen with a paint drying fast, and I had lost my stick. With that ballpoint, I found another layer of texture. The pen bleeds into the ink allowing a "Van Goghish" sort of visceral presence.

Painting with nail polish is more permanent than watercolor, even though I still mix the two, and I admit a set of good, colored pens helps to work edges and shadows. It makes a painting that doesn't fade back to bone, or a friend fade into nowhere, dust, one who is "just gone."

I told Gloria I didn't want any of Rudy's burned-up body. Instead, I wanted one of his dress shoes. Preferably his black, left, dress shoe since he can't wear it anymore, and I mentioned that I planned to paint it with fingernail polish, then hang it on the wall in my office and know he is still walking with me, that it will hurt a bit because he's only wearing one shoe. He will be with me until I'm gone. I refuse to allow him to become a haunting sketch of my memory.

Gloria, his wife, was my seventh grade English teacher, so she's the one you can blame for all the poems. She taught me how to write at an early age. And blame my wife for consistently remaining my reason to wake every morning and go to bed every night. She is my muse for writing as well as for painting. She's the one who said, "I think a totem pole is a great idea," and she has the wisdom to tell me often, "Go paint or clean the house."

Also, one last important thing, cats are a lot less likely to walk across a nail polish painting while it's still wet. I guess it's the smell. Still, Boogie Dew sits in my lap while I paint and tells me when it's time to go back inside.

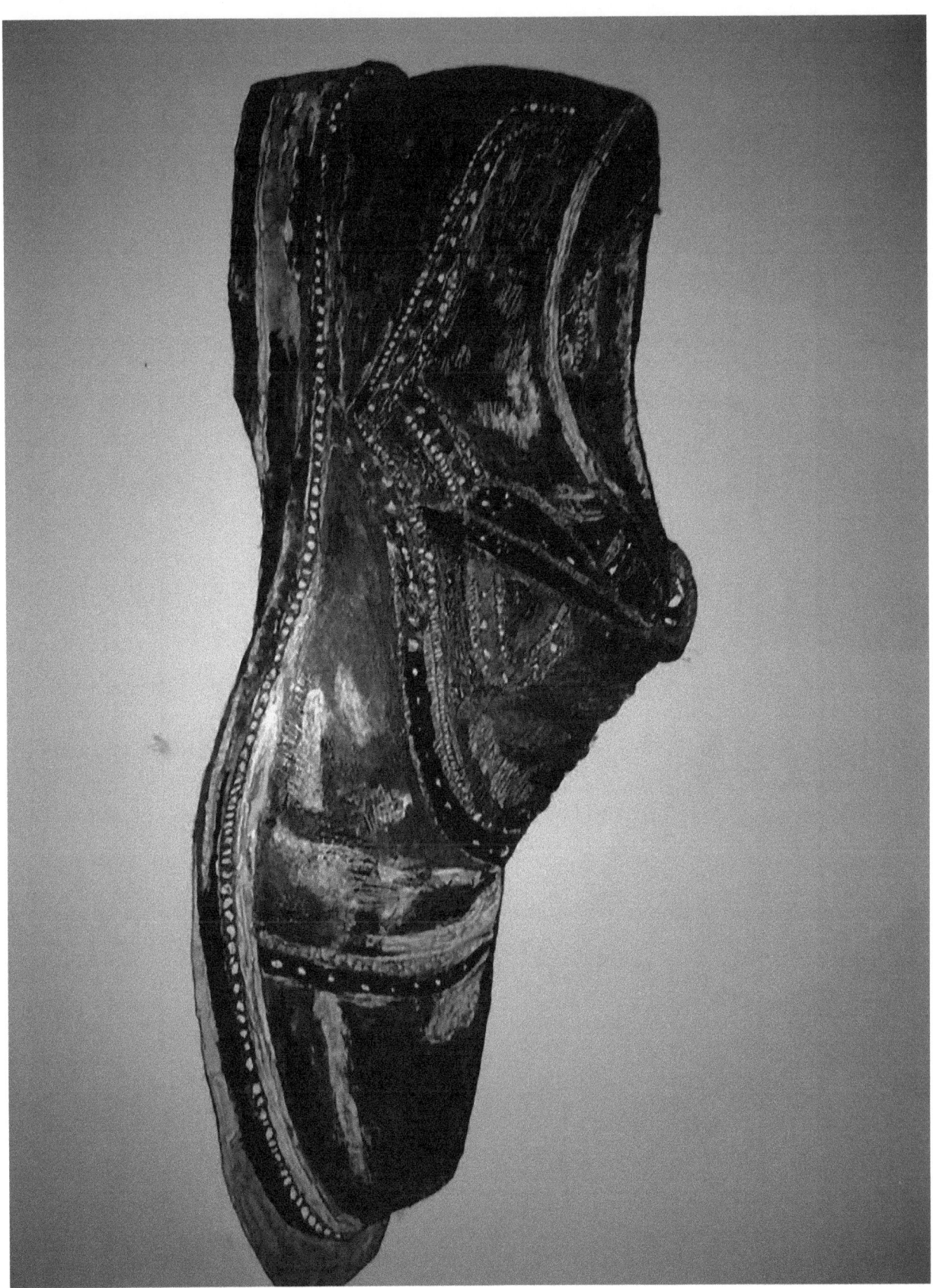

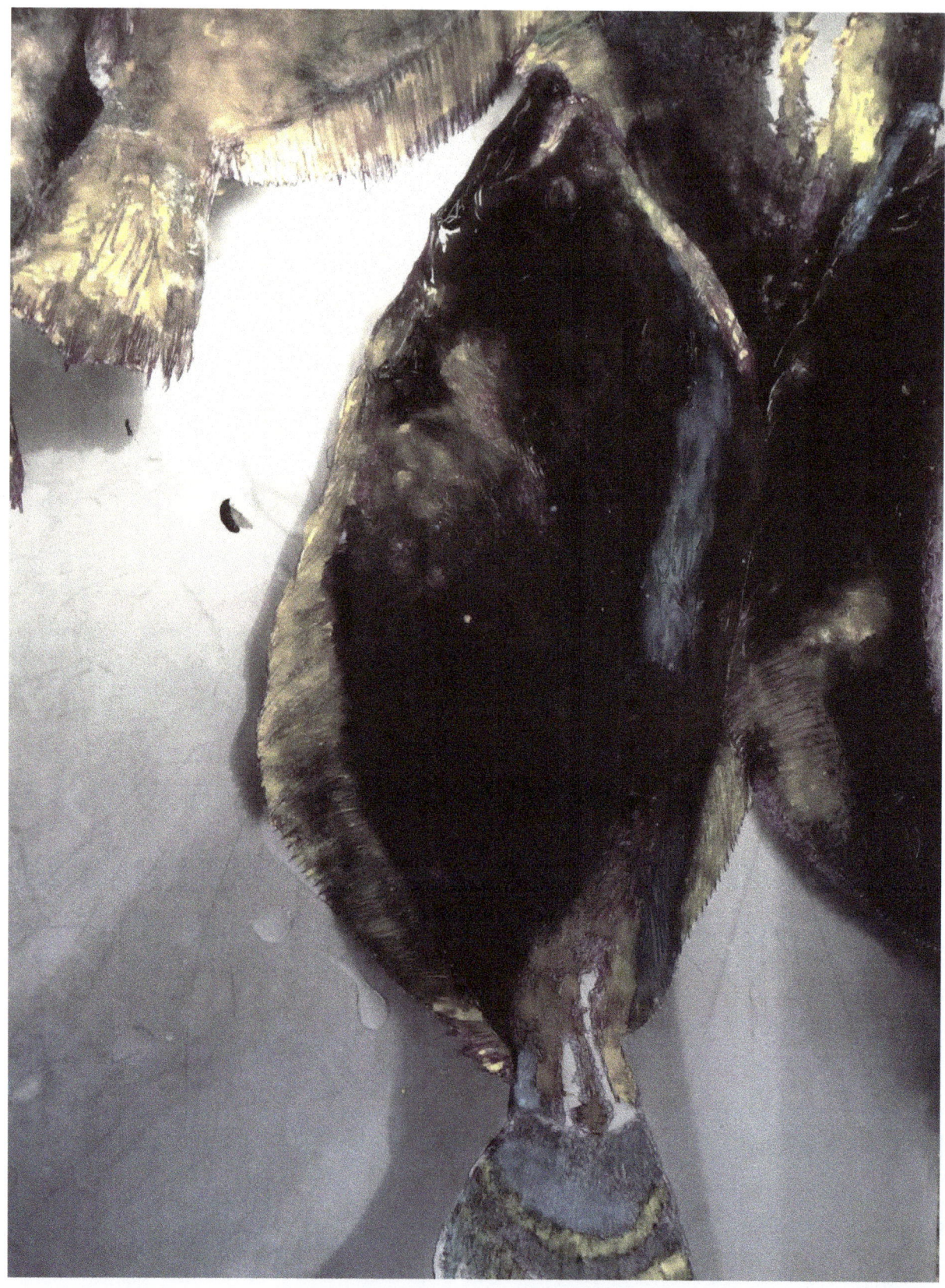

Floundering Lesson from an Oldest Brother in Matagorda Bay

You don't just grab a pointy object and drive
to the ocean's edge and aimlessly wallow
in water with a Walmart flashlight at midnight.

The process requires a brother: one who has walked
knee-deep in life, out of the boat, across the bay, not
fearing falling in that unseen channel, or that hidden barb
of a Ray, or Jellyfish trying to wrap lovingly around a leg;

It takes a brother, smart enough to carry underwater lamps
to light the way, patience, knowing the right direction,
in the right shoes that keep me above the almost knee deep
silt, encouragement—a lack of pride—to let me miss
the first flounder to gig and string, to sacrifice one mistake
to let me learn how to harvest the rest of the fruitful game;
then, the boat strategically waiting at the end to plane across the bay,
where he backs the trailer, loads, and pulls out in one fluid motion.

Loading the boat would have taken me half a day.
It took him less than four minutes.

He coaches me as he cleans the fish; I don't get to clean—not yet:
that is an art. He points me to return the sacrificed
carcasses, bones and fins, to the waiting gars rolling
the water beside the dock. "Watch," he says. I do.
The carcasses catch and shift then abruptly disappear:
A table cloth pulled from under a set table leaving nothing disturbed.

Only after he slides me into bed, do I start
to understand the journey he has been on to get
to this point of his life beside rising reeds
silhouetted against a full moon under
the silent stars riddling their constellations.

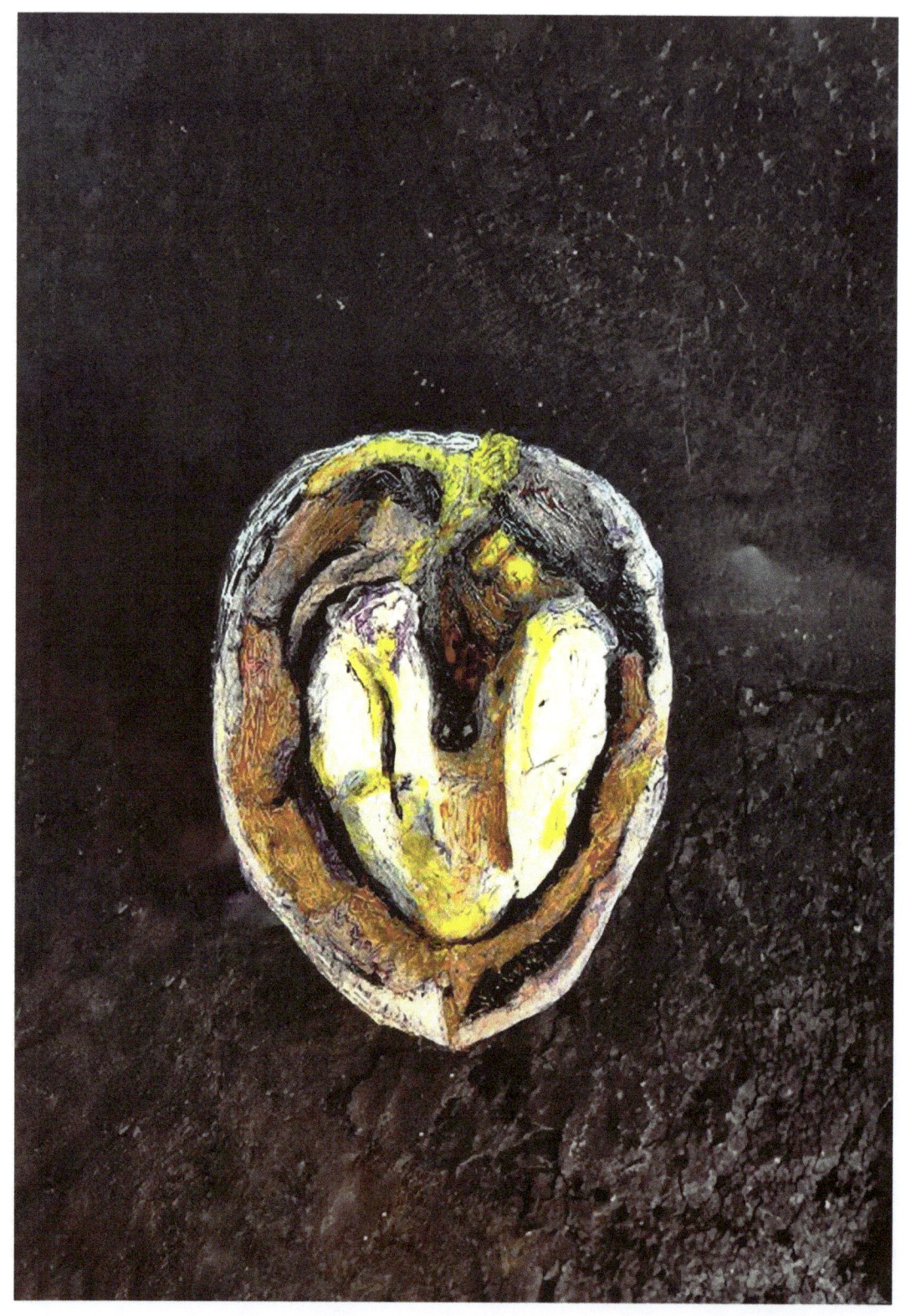

Keith's Cancer

Keith was skeet shooting when that
"walnut-sized" brain tumor brought
him to a babble. His trigger finger
stopped. He tried to reboot, over
and over, but he is stuck in time now,
trying to mouth his new name.

We are reborn when we look
through death's mask. Crack

a walnut, look at the intricate pattern,
the meat, winding protein, packed, no room
for even one more twist in any compartment.

Keith joked, "Cancer is a Bachelorette party arriving
in Vegas. At the airport, the cell arrives, immediately
begins splitting into clicks, succinctly spilling its
contents into taxies and limos—it wants to cover all
demographics, no prejudice—elevators up and down
into rooms, twisting into the beds like
screws, emerging recharged into hallways to
red kisses in corners, sidewalk to streets
to crossroads; finally, it hubs out to wheel at the
airport to every dark ragged-edged corner of the
spinning globe—the host."

I guess we can call it what it is, then—"Cancer." Keith
has cancer that the doctor is trying to steal from his open
skull while he is awake, trying to corral it
without stealing Keith's memory remembering.

What will he dream tonight behind that locked
door? Clay targets flying across his blue eyes? That one
missed, that one that fell, just beside that Mesquite,
that one that cracked the red clay of his life, that one
reposing under the July Texas sun, his missed
mark, slowly rooting his final seed back into the soil?

Or will he dream of his simple soul breathed
back into God's ever, waiting for his wife Mary's arms,
his son tooting his Tuba into each ticking second.

Jesus and Muhammad

Jesus' locker is just beside Mohammad's
at Sara Issac's Elementary in Plano, Texas.

In Miss Rule's class, they both sit, "Crisscross-Applesauce,"
during circle, draw their "A, A, A, Alligator"
and feed "A, A, A, Albert" the Guinea Pig on the way out
to recess. They get a lesson from a third grader on how
to dump neophytes off the see-saw. At lunch
they barter for chocolate milk; Muhammad trades
a hot dog for Jeff's green beans. Just
boys being boys. By day three they both

have a crush on Mary, the new girl.

The forbidden is delicious when you are young.
Suppressing desire is a grown man's work.

During free time, Mohammad builds pillars,
between blocks and tables, then
Jesus turns them over in a tantrum.

At nap time once, lying between them,
Mary swore her headache just "went away."

Just, kids being kids.

In Jr. High, the boys both just seemed
a bit lost at first, trying to find out
if the football team needed them or
the band their dissonant notes. They
ended-up partners on the debate team.

They became great orators and mutually
appreciated Mary's growing breasts and
budding girlfriends, who, by summer break,
were laying half-naked in the sun, just out of the pool,
wet, reddish skin with white flashes of secret creases,
on the hot concrete, with that rain on dry dust smell.

Remember when all the smells and the colors of the world
were still straight tube unmixed oil on canvas?

At graduation, they promised to call
each other from college, but they didn't.

In fact, they watched in disbelief as their
world, once sitting parallel, side-by-side,
was sliced, knife sharp, in half, a pomegranate,
with seeds of humanity to be consumed.

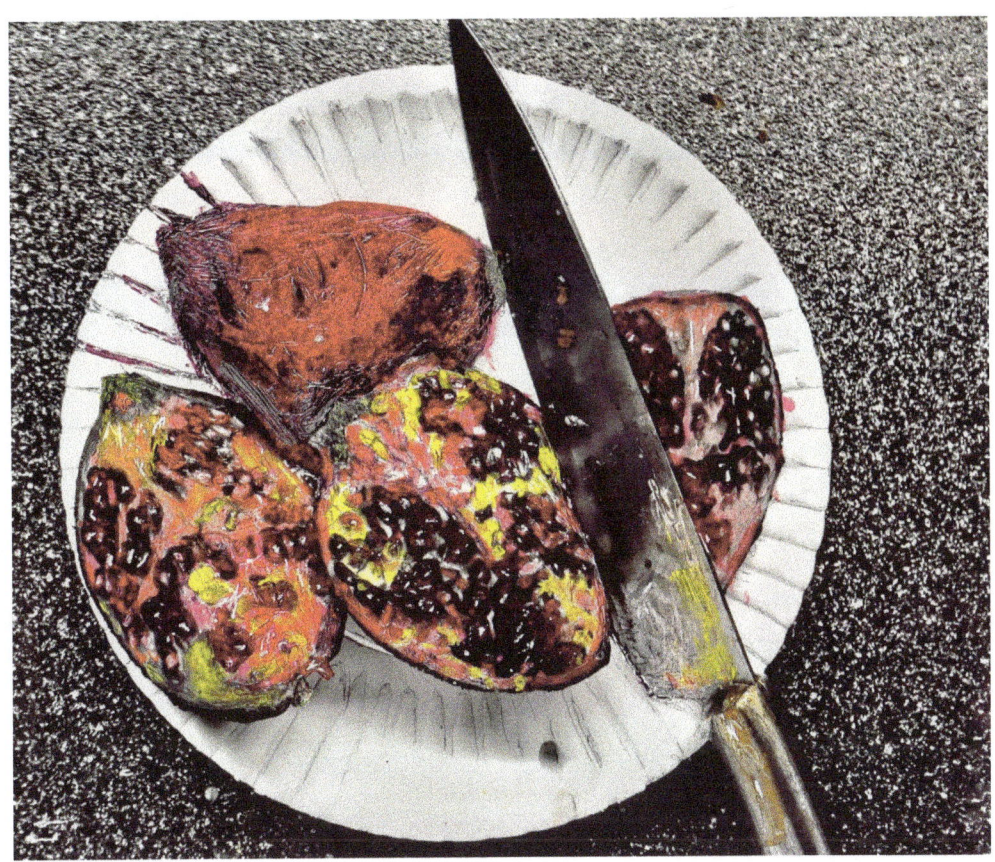

At the Reservation: Sunrise Keeper

Grandfather passed me every morning in the darkness,
by my cot on the porch, not even careful to be quiet.
One morning, six years old, I secretly
followed him over the trail, between
the foothill trees; he crawled
over rocks in a certainly certain order,
and finally sat, face raised
to the sky on his stone slab worn
smooth from this daily ritual.

The sky began to stir its stars in its black, then
added the red fan spreading, followed by orange;
next the yellow eye peeked over that line,
pulling a canvas of blue, clear as my first
grade teacher's eyes. It was a new day.

"Halito. Ya-ta-hay," he said smiling, just
as the sun broke yellow yolk.

"Ya-ta-hay" is a greeting; I'm not "Injun" stupid.

"I know you are there," he said. I didn't know if
he meant the sun or me. "I am the keeper
of the sun. The sun will not rise without me." He added,
"We all die and are born again each morning,"

He turned and looked me directly in the eye and I had to look away.

"Tomorrow, stay in bed and make the world dark," I challenged.

I crawled from behind the bush I thought I was hiding in.
I really wanted to see his power. He became
agitated. "Why would I want to prove
to you I can make the world dark only to sacrifice
light to the rest of the world." I was swarmed,
a hornet's nest of thoughts stinging the turns of my brain.

We never spoke of "it" again.

At my son's birth, by the vending machine
he asked me, "Do you still want
to see the world dark?"

I smiled him a simple, "Never." He returned
my smile and invited me to bring
my son to watch the sun rise—"Soon."
I did. Three generations watching
the sunrise in silence. Three days
later he passed away.

At the Giving Ceremony, Don, my oldest brother got
his Speaking Stick. Steve got his cedar Hope Chest
he made for Grandmother Icy. I got his worn leather bag.
As I curiously looked inside, I found a note:
"Today, the sun did not rise. The sun
is yours to rise now; without you, it will not."

Dead Animal Game

Most children count the color of cars, punch "Slug Bugs,"
or are the first to call "Pancaters" from the back seat of
the Mercury at the sight of those distant lights of a small
town wrapped in the black blanket of night.
My children count dead animals, keeping a log.

Armadillos usually win in Spring. Skunks, a close second.
Squirrels win in town, sadly—along with cats. Dogs, fewer
than you would think; chickens more common than
you would think in rural America. Deer are overwhelming
winners during Central Texas mating season. I once

suggested the children count mattresses blown off minivan
roofs, aluminum ladders, Igloo coolers, carpet remnants—
objects that don't feel; objects that don't remind us of loss,
or absurdity, of crossroads with blind-eyed, tunnel vision chasing
the one "she" down the road you wish you *had* challenged.

My son once even started a "Never Seen by the Public" list.
His 'baby anteaters'—were possums; then there was Jenni's
Tarantula migration by Abilene: hundreds mashed
into starfishes with eight legs. The winner? York's, two
blue crabs squished on South Padre's causeway making a,

"Medusa Washing Dishes." That Monday night, just out
of San Angelo's city lights toward Sterling City, my son got
one simple word out: 'Deer!" Eyes in the headlights,
mirrored back, then it jumped, one bolt, sliding across
the windshield, glass breaking over Jenni's ducked head;

it vaulted over the roof and hit sliding in a slow rotation,
no movement. Our headlight's cross-eyed into the sky, spinning
across asphalt hard though barbed-wire-out-of-tune-to a stop in the
barrow ditch next to a Santa Gertrudis; she—instead of running—
came to investigate, perhaps a new mother. An eighteen wheeler

swerved to miss, almost hitting an oncoming Silverado. [Most
people are killed by the kicking hooves of the animal frightened,
trapped inside its mechanical coffin.] We all checked fine. Darkness
now, nowhere, I ran and pulled the heavy deer by his leg to the side,
"To swerve would—" his final breath hissed from his red open belly.

My daughter came to me crying, then my son in simple silence.
We sat beside the deer, his broken rack of years, neat bone honed
on brush. The other side rack was splintered bleached
bone, like conduit. "We should kiss it," Jenni said. I thought that
was reasonable. I nodded. She did. My son did. In silence,

I did, three times: threes and sevens are lucky. I checked
the car, put water from the creek running parallel
in the radiator, filled the cooler with more; it started.
We left, one headlight spraying its question into the sky,
our wounded mechanistic beast, lurching in hurt spurts,

radiator hissing steam, the yellow blood of coolant spilling
an oily rainbow reflecting Dali's full melting moon. Sterling City
was just "Pancakers" away; Jenni brushed a bit more of the glass
from under her dress. "Dad? Can you turn on the light?" I did.
"Uncontested winner!" The recorder of truth always in the back seat.

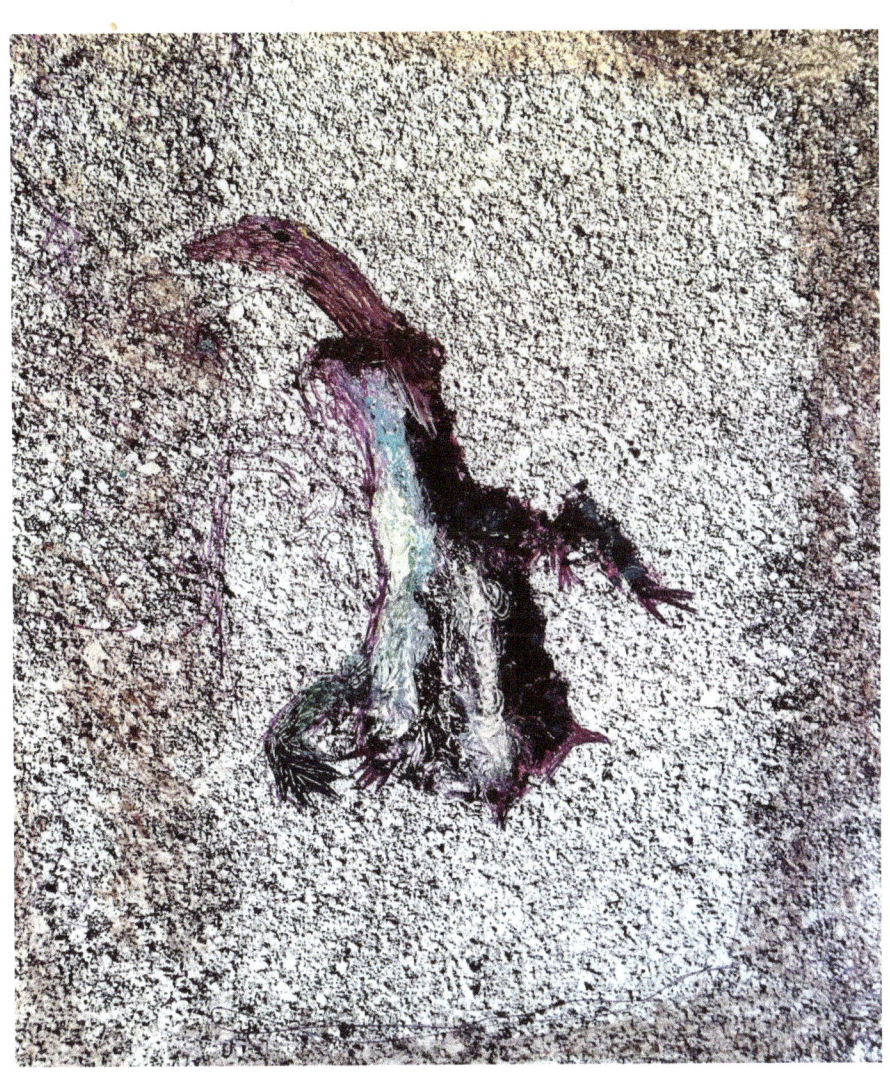

Playing Bridge at the Nursing Home

The call from the nursing home always comes
in the middle of the night from someone you
don't know, to tell you, "She doesn't have that
much time left."   Then, there's the silent twelve hour
car ride to the Bridge Game. All the relatives simply
showing up like "ante," letting
everyone know they are "in." The oldest daughter
begins with a bold bid: "One No Trump." "Everyone carry
your own weight. Simply do the right thing." But
there are too many cards. The middle brother bids weak,
"Two Spade." He wants to discuss the burial. The youngest
brother skips Hearts and ups to "Three Diamond:" the house
his daughter could use, new carpet, his medical bills, and
that he's taken "care of her mostly, anyway."

The mother suddenly becomes an old pair of pants with
hidden change stuffed in that watch pocket on
the right side no one ever uses.

"Three No Trump." The daughter fists her cards
to her mouth and bets that she can finesse
the older brother's King of Hearts with her
Jack and then follow with her Queen and her Ace.
She is void in Diamonds. The Brother-in-Law gladly lays
down his cards in four lines, red-black,
and comments he's glad he doesn't have to play
this hand and pops the tab of his Michelob. "It's
good to be the Dummy," he states the obvious.

After, there's the silent twelve-hour car ride back
to everyday to wait for the call from the nursing
home, the one that will come while you are at work on the
third day of your new job and you'll talk to someone—
maybe one of your brothers—and they will tell you
she is gone and that she didn't suffer much.

Bridge might be better if the two Jokers were
left in the deck. Otherwise it's rather predictable, isn't it?

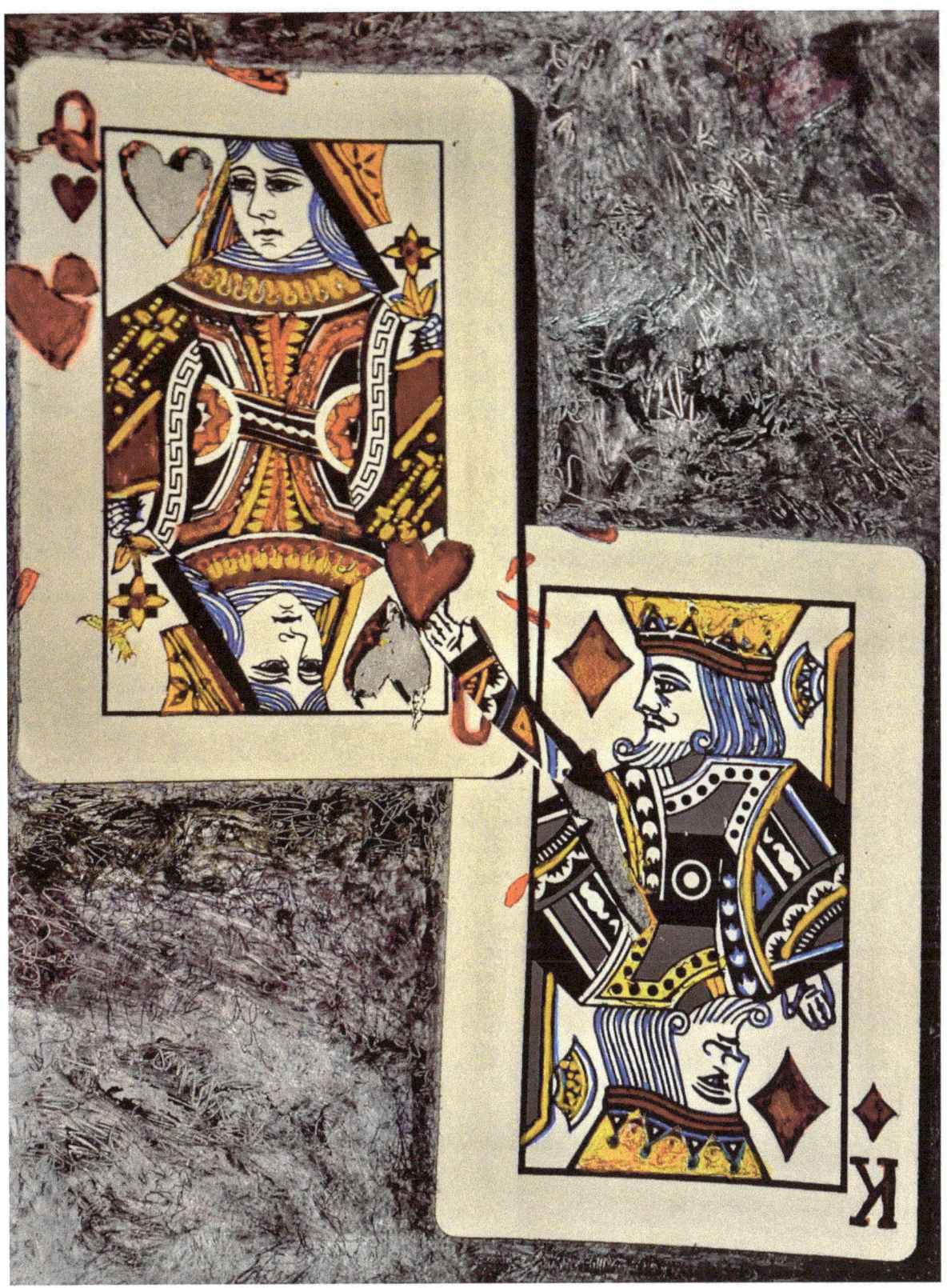

Coyote and a Coupon

Tuesday a Coyote bounded the fence and tail-
chased Martin, my cat, of thirteen years, circle
burning around the shed. Martin stood ground
one final second; then, my banshee wife spilled

from the house in full-chord. Martin clawed,
hip-toe-hunch-and-thrust up the tree; the coyote
leapt gracefully over the four-foot fence. My job
was to climb the twenty-foot extension ladder with

two, two by four's screwed together long ways
and get the cat. We saved Martin, a cat taken
for granted like we do God. Like the wife in bed
next to you. Two days later the Coyote

choked the cat. I saw it. I was able to get
him to drop the body before leaping the fence.
I was witness to some animal planet moment
but this was real. I went to the lumber yard, got cedar,

built a coffin—it was too small. Then, a second
too large to fit into the hole because I had hit
bedrock. I decided to bury Martin like my father
said he wanted to be buried: "Bare and in the dirt,

nostrils filled with the clay that built us."
I concede. He'll feed flowers and maybe
even be dug up like a King Tut God some day.
I even put a tunic on him and a can of Fancy Feast.

He *was* a good God. I placed heavy bricks
on top of the soil to discourage any disturbing.
I also dusted him with insecticide. I showered.
We put clean sheets on the bed and the little

kitten who looked for him hour after hour
mewing high pitched mews finally curled
around us. The bricks the next morning
were moved, clawed out and Martin's body

was gone, the tenacious work ethic of the
Coyote. Nature has its way of reminding

us that we are not in charge. We are not
the center of the bull's-eye; we are but one

small cog in a seemingly mechanical
universe ruled by God and absurdity,
regeneration, and memory. I put the
cat food coupon on the refrigerator.

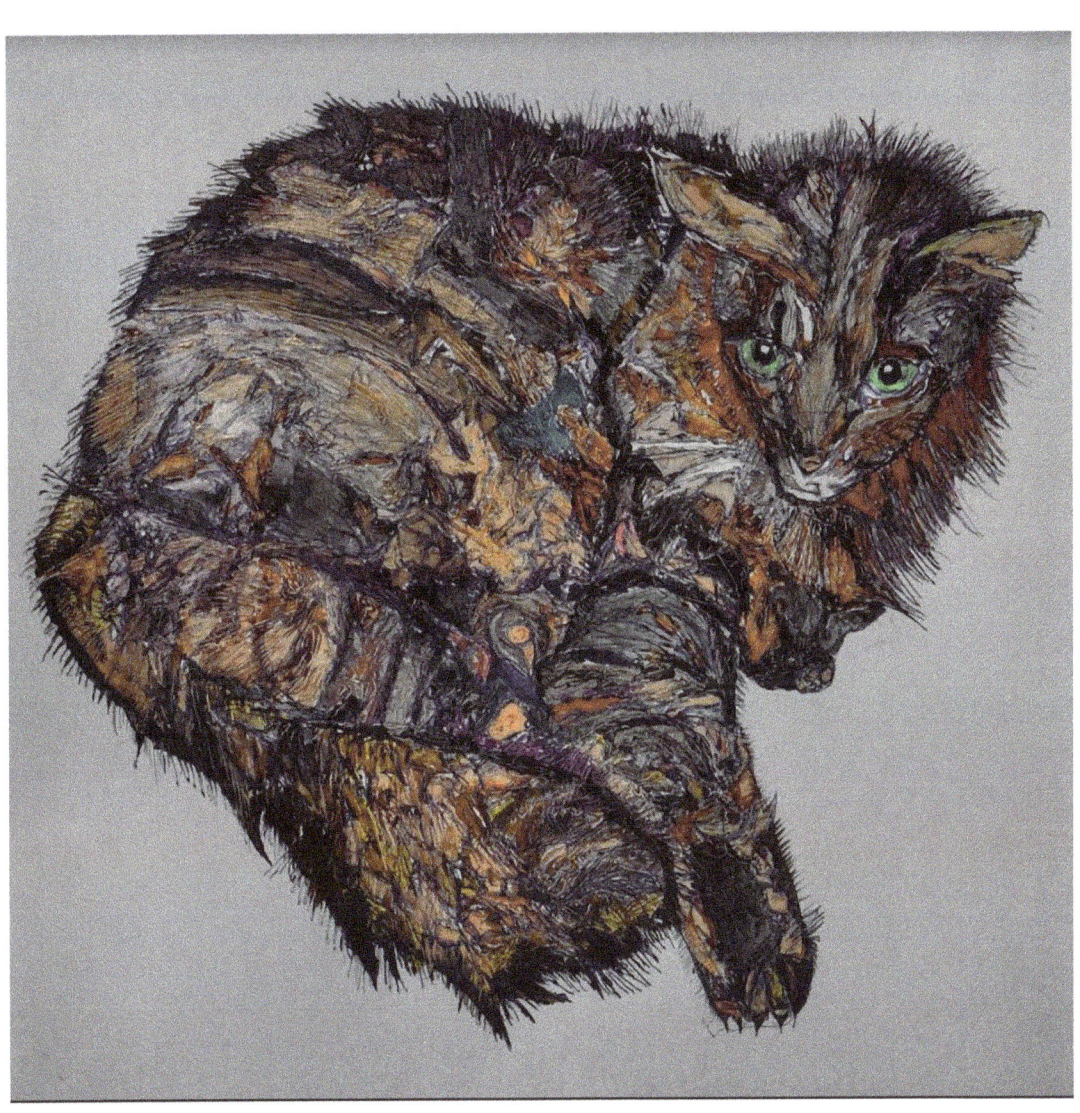

Ode to Carol Coffee Reposa's "Full-Stop" on Her Typewriter and Why I Prefer Pencils

I noticed the "Full-stop" period
on her last letter. Her manual typewriter
leaves the center of the period clear,
like a very small, full moon,
like the circle revolving around
our friendship.

We have agreed, in our
older years to quit
seeing lines.

She once asked *why* I prefer
composing in pencil. I replied,
"Because I can break it
when the words won't come
out of the lead and find them inside."

Her last, hand-typed
note with each struck
letter and hand-signed
finish makes me return
to my pencils of varied length,
some broken, to mine the lead for that
illogical belief that

anyone will ever want
our words as
much as we do.

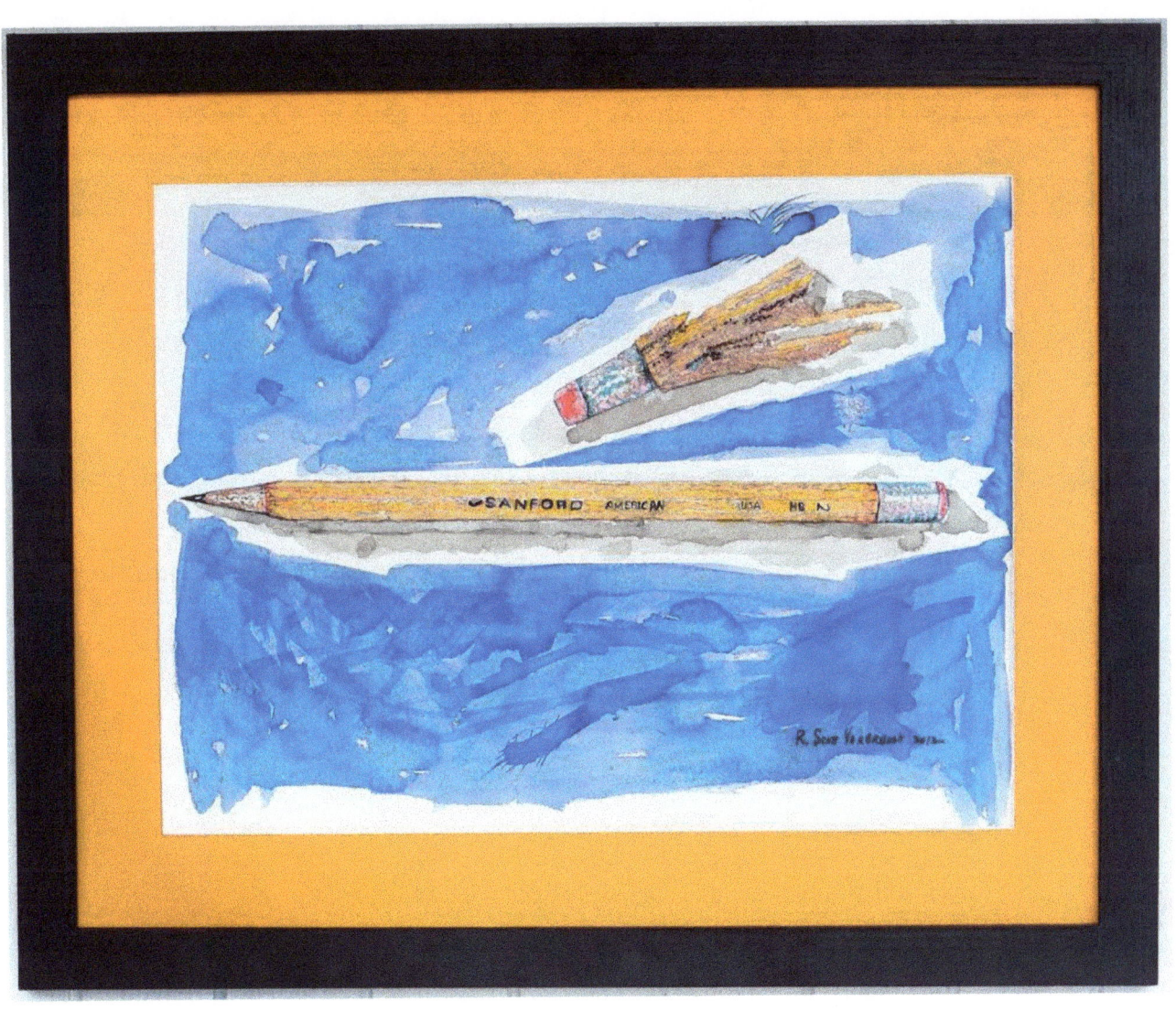

Remember That Morning Just after Dawn?

You were angry. I start with that
because that Cardinal just outside
the window raising his voice was calling
for her, over and over, waiting, listening,
no response and he tried again and again.

You are in bed. Naked under white sheets. You
said, "Will you go tell him it's Saturday, so we can go
back to sleep?" Then, the sun rose a bit more.

I listened for her to answer him, knowing that
would take him to her, away from our window.
No answer. I reach over to feel the heat of the bed,
the fire between our bodies. At least she didn't pull away.

We should not have fought last night. Let's don't do that.
You can keep the new kitten. I just had to put up a slight fight.

Try to be the girl bird listening;
I'm calling in every language I know.
I *know*. I'll shut up in a second, but

please keep reading this poem. Please keep the kitten
who fell on you from the tree at Bob Woodruff Park,
104 degrees, Coyote prints in the dirt all around the trunk.
Her stripped chaps, Calico, *Cowgirl Jesse*;

You had already named her before I even got home.

I felt her nuzzle and claw her way into my
life last night, too. She even tried to nurse
my neck for a bit before falling asleep
hanging on like a new charm. The girl Cardinal answered.

Go back to sleep. Remember that silence after
Cowgirl finally slept and my sheets finally
rested, and that we don't have to go to work
today and that we will be on that jet
in a few days after coffee and cream and a quiet
morning watching her show-off, running the length
of the couch and beating up her new
rooster toy and the sun moving deliberately
across the sky, just as he always does, Apollo
at the reigns, whipping wildly or pulling

the reigns to get to sunset at just the right time,
his six horses' hooves, bleeding the sunset red.
Most days we don't notice that we get to start over
with a new sun and a new life, fresh skin, finally kisses
and no words, but the distant calling of that bird
in song of him searching for her.

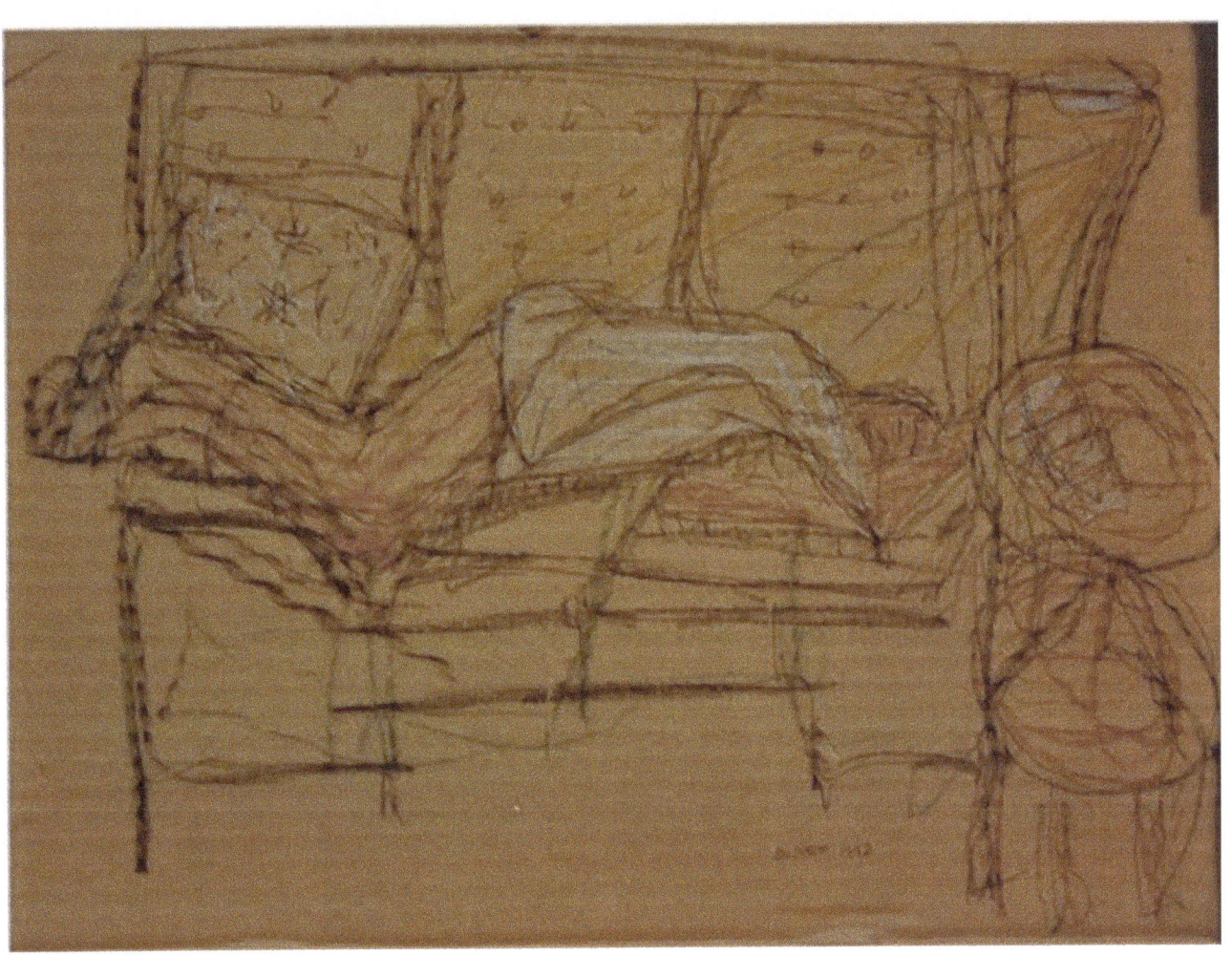

Palate Man: Keeper of Right Turns
for Jason McMenamy

I drove my daughter to school each day. She—obsessive
compulsive disorder—counted and made
every turn a milestone. At the end
of our block, at the "tomato red" stop sign,
is a man who moves palates for a living.

We honk. He waves, exact and sure
as a cuckoo clock. "That's 'Palate Man,'" she said
in a voice like announcing a superhero.

Every day, never missing, the conjunction became a pattern,
a black-and-white square floor, an autumn's leaf firmly
snuggled into winter's first snowy floor. Palate man became a place.

"How many palates were in his truck today? How
many would he deliver? Would he park crooked,
or have them stacked in odds or evens?" She always
questioned. Palate Man *never* varied.

Palate Man is a superhero in my comic book, saving
my counting girl who yearns simply *to do* labor as a daily task,
instead of her day *being* labor. Because

Palate Man always waves. Palate Man always
acknowledges our vehicle. Palate Man can stack
Babel up to heaven and never be one inch off
the square of perfect right angle measure, ever, never-ever.

This year she announced her Halloween costume: "Palate Man."
We cut a palate in half and she trudged inside it, arms out in
a crucifix holding her plastic pumpkin, always announcing herself in a
Robotic superhero voice, "I am 'Palate Man.'" I forwent explaining.

Once home I asked her, "Why Palate man?" She answered,
"He is my favorite right turn," as she started lining Halloween
candy in squares with perfect right angles in groups of three.

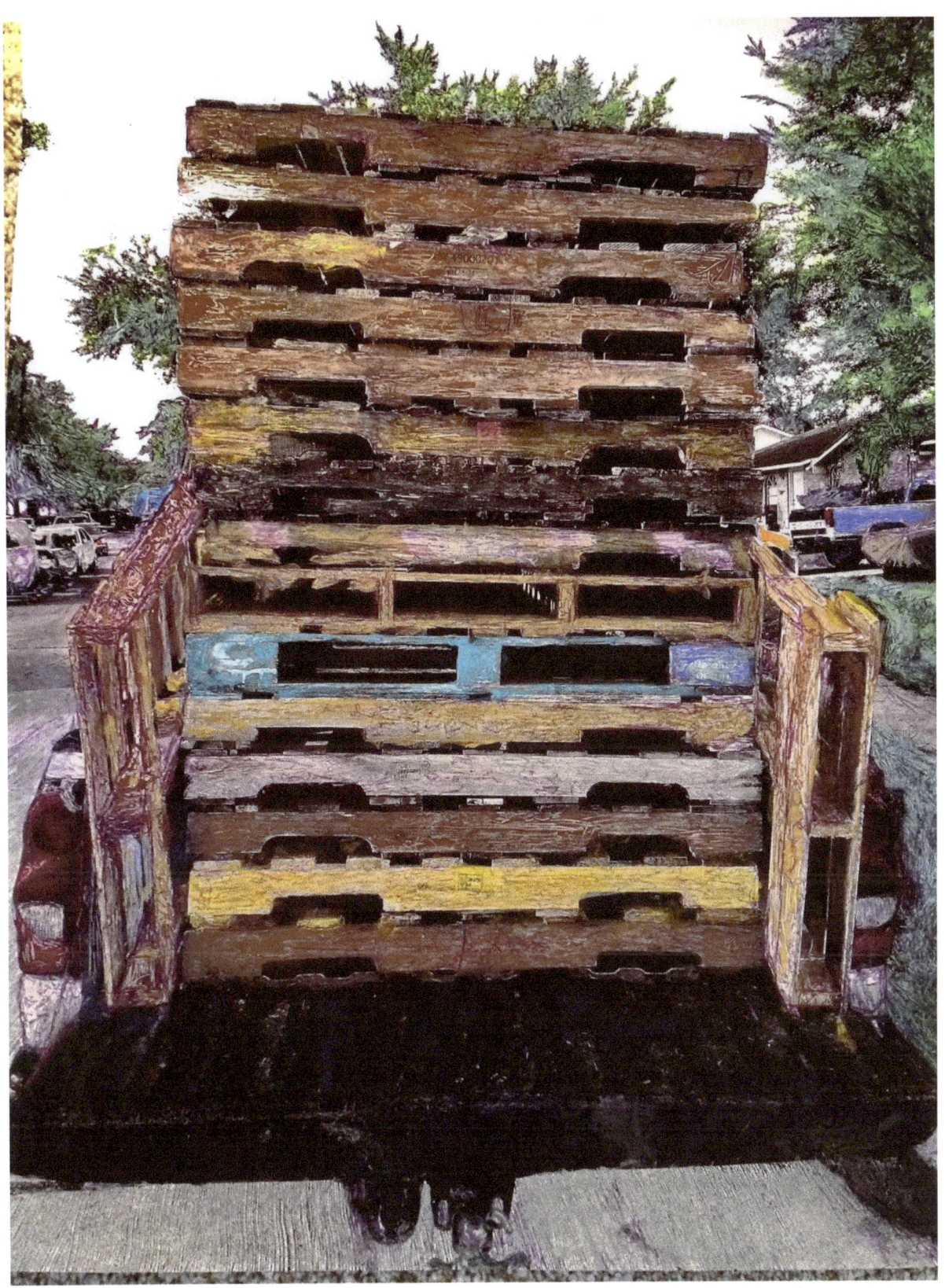

My First Southwest Flight

Mother's mother lived in Panhandle; we in Levelland.
Once a year we piled in the Fairlane 500. Mother
started her rules to be followed just outside the city limits:
the Interstate. "No sliding down the Oak banister.

Make sure the water in the Matuss wine bottle
in the refrigerator wasn't really wine." Sometimes it was.
Creamed potatoes with a scooped out spoonful on top filled
with melted butter, were Pawpaw's. Our reward: clean

Clorox sheets, crisp as a white lighting strike, sun dried; when
I shattered my collar bone, Evel Knievel on my Schwinn, Dad and
Mom had to work. My injury became a long distance rotary phone
dial that ultimately smack-kissed my first flight on a plane. I was seven;
my virgin flight. Imagine the wonder, the newness of that moment.

No century of humans before us had ever flown; *we* discovered it. Once

on, the stewardess asked who would be willing to take
responsibility for me: half of the plane lifted an arm. I ended
between two smoking businessmen. They wiggled me to the window seat.
The take off lifted us over Palo Duro Canyon under the left
wing; I imagined painted Buffalo, running its edge, with

crayon painted Indians arching their bows and wondering if red
was the blood of the river? That gave way to pointed squares
of white cotton, open bolls, marked against irrigation pipes with
long arms of hollow steel painting the brown square in a bright green circle,
just beside yellow fields: like an organized eye-shadow compact kit.

I was a tiny 'god' seeing the world as one place instead
of a point of departure and destination. I suppose God

likes looking down more than up, and how gracious of God to allow
us to see that Godly view even for just a moment before landing
us back to earthly duties. Image the years it took to dig,
with river and wind, that Palo Duro Canyon; then know, *it took longer*
for us to rise on wings out of this material world to see it from above.

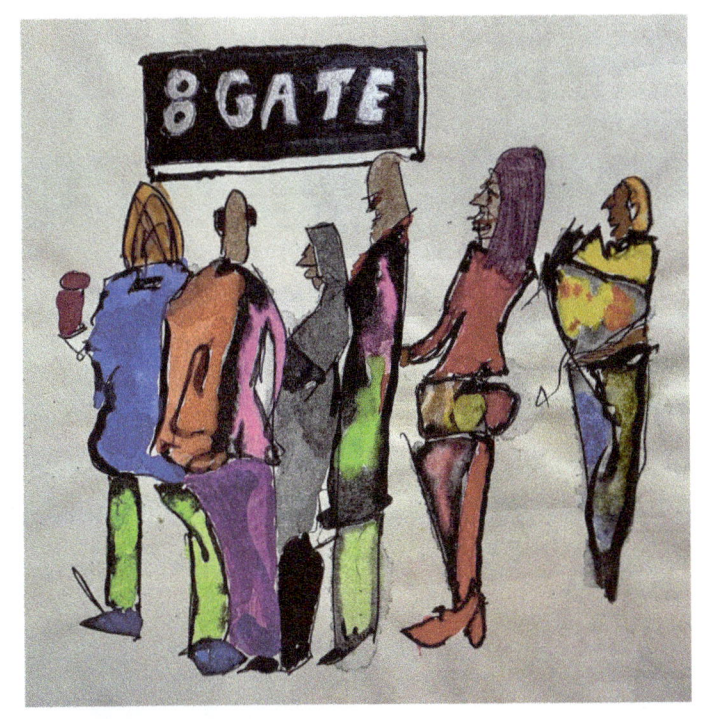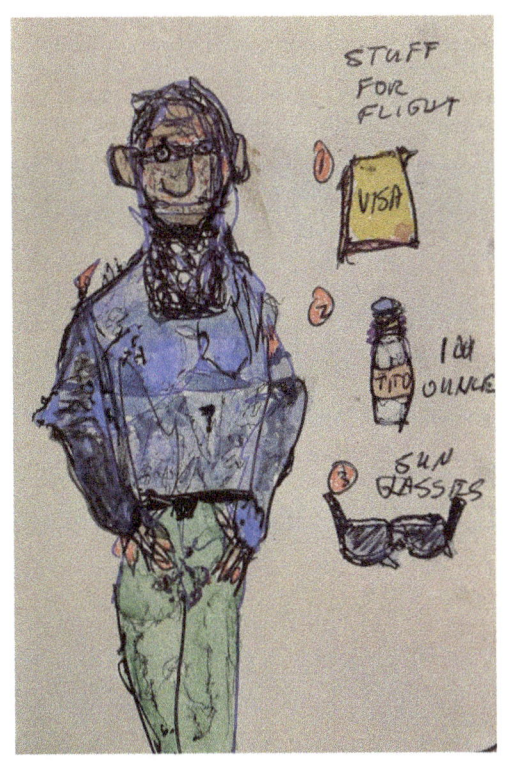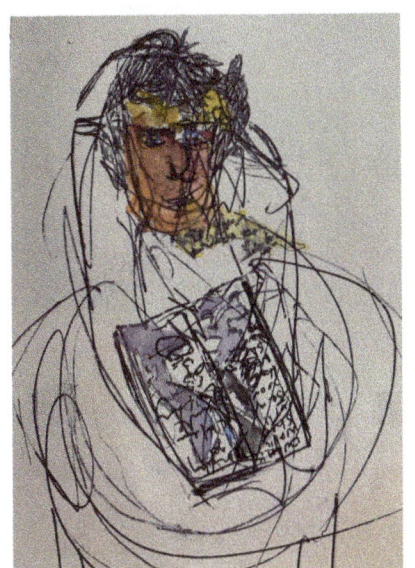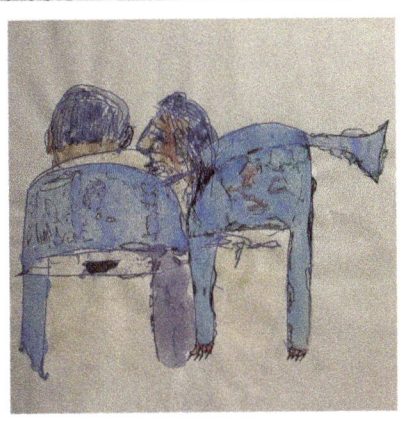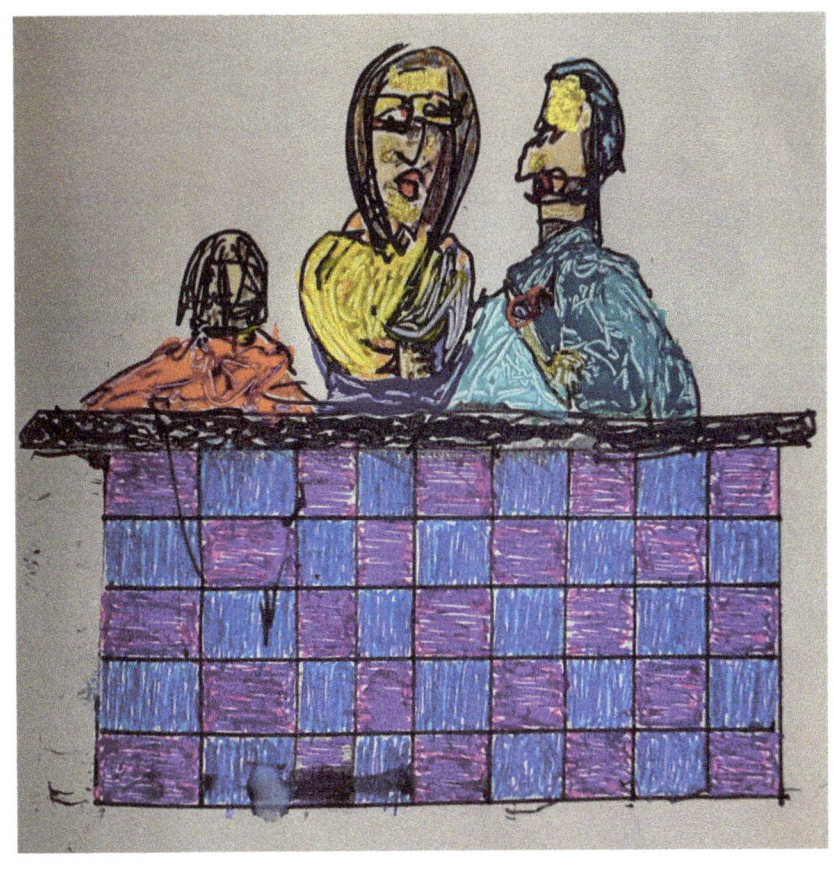

Ataxia
For Emily

I first met her when she was not telling,
when she could still walk, without anyone
noticing that slight hitch in her left leg,
or that speck of slurred speech, that she
could cover with a laugh and say, "You know?"

The same way I lean against the blackboard during
lecture just to take one second off my dying hips.

Watch the sun rise—*once*. Get up before it does.
Notice how the cherry and orange and lemon push
the black, then pour mixed color into the daily window of morning.

It's really rather quick—like the first time.

Then, watch the sun set. It falls,
leaving its orange slices, pulp
held to light with rind opaque.

Otherwise, all day, it just seems to hang "Guernica—
Picasso- light-bulb" over that wrenching, bellowing bull.

Emily found out she had **Ataxia** . . . something, during
her last years of high school. It is terminal.

Does finally naming something make "it" more bearable?
Doesn't naming "it," make "it" mortal, too?

Her life became fast motion to me; slow
to her. She is the travelling sun
now and I watch each slice of her fall
over the horizon in pieces into dark;
seconds on a watch, wishing for her that
one lost hour of ennui that comes with age, that
I-don't-want-to-go-to-work-today look. But in her, all
I see is the *now* of yesterday, and I feel guilty
I just wasted thirty minutes watching the nightly news
so I could be caught up on the day's horrid handywork of humanity.

Emily, is the child chasing
the singing popsicle truck, fisting
her dollar bill for a fruit-filled *Red Freeze*.

But notice her timer has started:
eat or *melt* or *time* it perfectly,
calculate the final bite without
dropping it to the hot concrete
to ooze uneaten in the sun,
food for those ants and their sticky shoes.

We all die. I just hope for those I love,
it is popsicle clean. Only the stick
left on the asphalt to bleach
in the sun: no sticky leftover mess,
or army of ants to take us away, piece
by piece, a simple last bite moment
in the healthy hot sun standing beside
the popsicle truck of our youth.

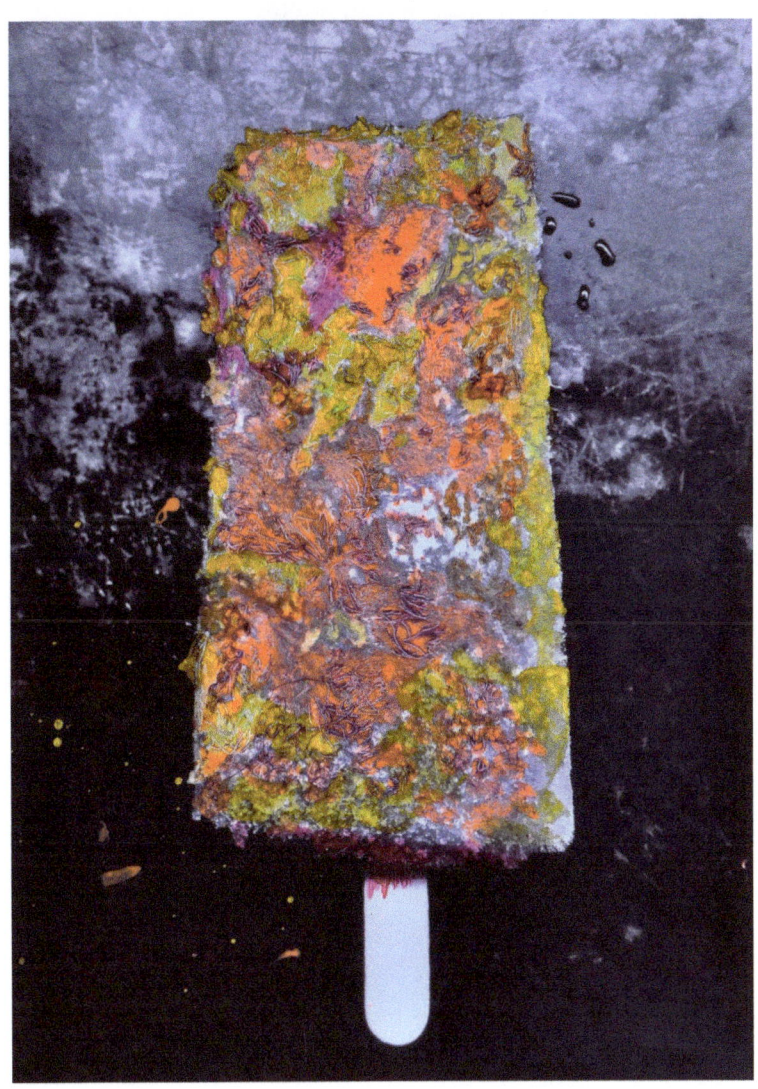

Upon Filling the Recycling Bin

Imagine, first, a seed watered to green sprout,
with that bulb already on top, ready to pop red,
in a few months, the yellow-black, fuzzy-backed bees, spreading
pollen around to the newlings. But, the world freezes, too.

Then, we are pressed flat between
pages and hidden on shelves to be future found,
and sometimes replanted, sometimes as seeds blown,
or salvaged, perhaps caught in a corner of a raised bed,
or another yard, or lost under the footed wooding
of some Sylvia Plathian floor to allow resurrection,
or in that used car sold eventually by the Sextons.

Every generation flows into some next moment
as if they are the answer to *that* new moment.

They are not; they are just the new question.

Let's believe in that one Canadian goose who winged
to Texas from Canada, or those Monarch Butterflies
who survive to eat my apples, then move on like drunken
frat boys with oversized wings and wire feet, somehow
miraculously able to hang on to this spinning globe. Blue
Whales, we can't find, but who are too big to hide who call
from the deep, high pitched pleading
for us to pay attention. My kitten

just wrapped around my leg. That is what is supposed to happen
to you when you contemplate that which is too large.
"It" comes and finds you in a small, obvious container,
a purr and several licks and eventual sleep.

"Are we simply blocks? Pieces of a growing puzzle, forever
feverishly rebuilding ourselves to some unending masterpiece?
Do we simply couple and reproduce that-which-works-with-
that-which-doesn't in an ignorant restart Easy Bake oven,
good-and-evil, traveling to complete the whole? Are we an, ever,
never-ending moment, growing dark-and-day to become?

I hope so.

Then, I opened the compost bin and dumped
in banana peels, egg shells, and a bag of mowed grass.

I hate mowing.
It makes me think too much.

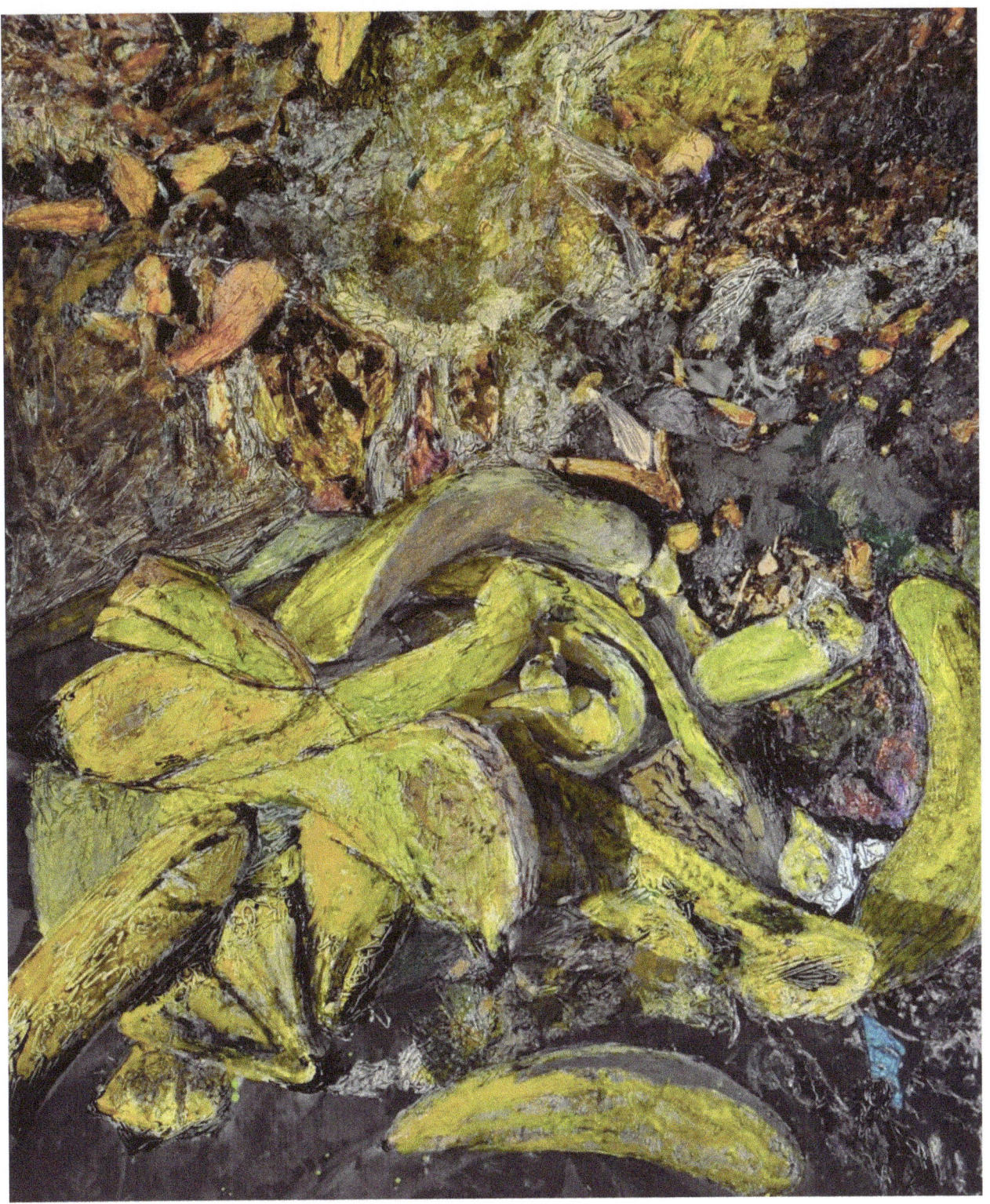

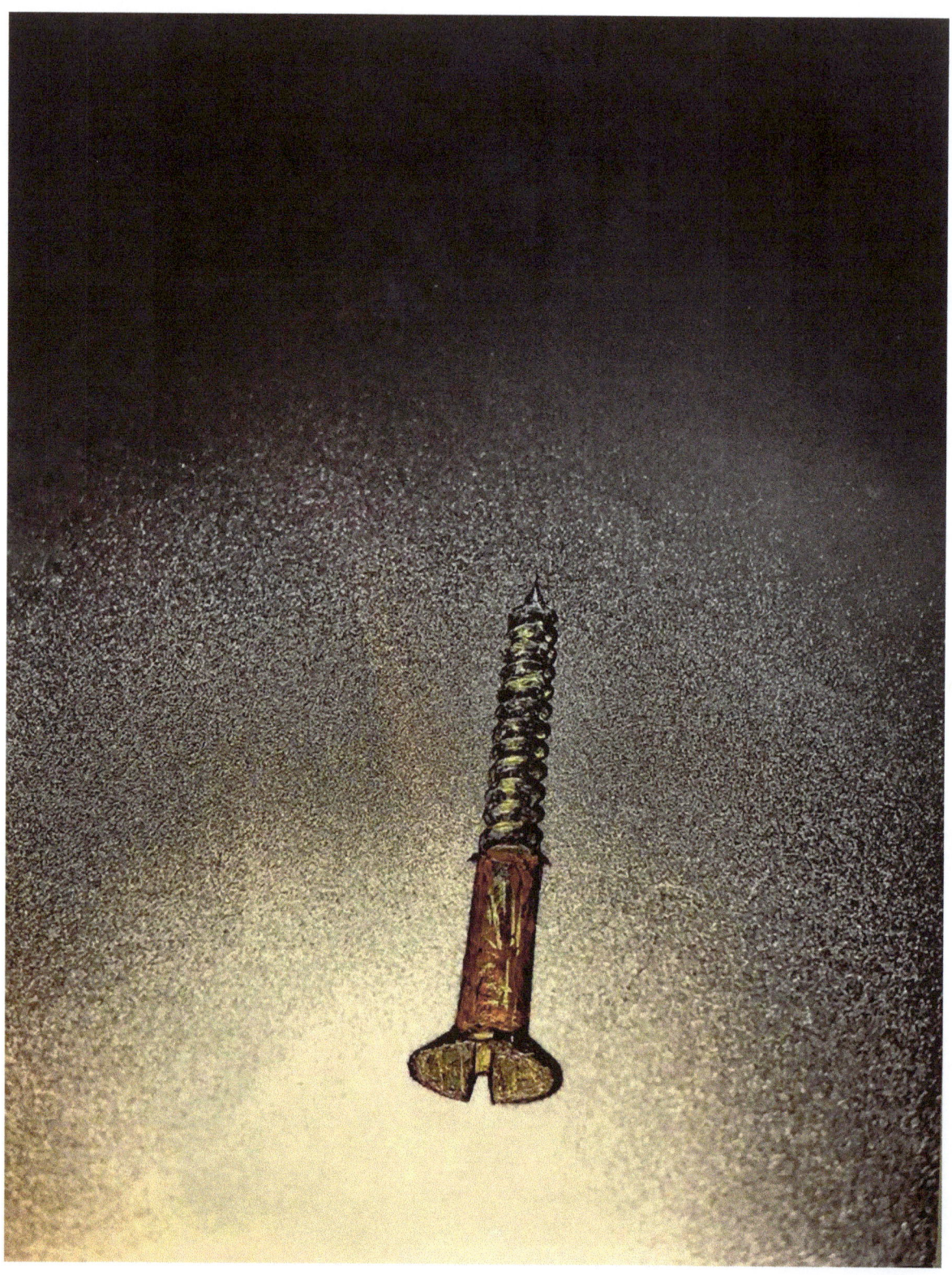

Thanksgiving Poem

Sherri's sister killed herself Thanksgiving morning,
in the garage, of her new house, in her new Audi.
She left the car running; he won't drive

that car or live in that house. She succeeded
in that part. My wife, as serious as I have
ever seen her, asked me, point-blank,

"Would you ever do something like that?"
I paused and responded truthfully, "No.
we have too much important in our garage."

Old license plates, half-empty paint cans, a broken leaf-blower,
stripped flat-head screws in jam jars, spider webs
too intricate, too important, too beautiful to destroy.

Chopping Cotton
For Kyle Wilkison

My brothers and I stood in the dark, like Mr. Reeder
said, and waited for his F-150 to rumble around the corner.
Dad got us this job to keep us out of trouble during summer.

Ten, eleven, and thirteen, hoes in hand, we tumbled
into the bed of Reeder's Blue Ford and caught one last sit
in the bed behind the back glass to the cotton rows stretching

from sunrise to sunset. It was my first day. We jumped bed
and sharpened our hoes. My father had a hoe all his life; I never
saw him sharpen it. That, was my first, "lessoning." Mr. Reeder

was straight and gruff, "Sixteen rows and then rest for five
minutes. Get a drink out of the barrow ditch." He watched
our first hour. My first mistake was chopping the actual cotton.

I got punched for that.

"Chop the *weeds*. Beasts standing alongside the cotton,
sharing their roots." After his sermon, Reeder left
to move pipe, and by noon the sand burned our bare feet.

We would rest them in the barrow ditch in the cold well-water
and get a drink by cupping our hands. Reeder's absence
allowed my brother to teach me the Clod Fight and Bull Snake

Throwing—although we all knew a Rattler was also fair game.
Rule was to throw the snake at the person most caught in their thoughts.
Bulls aren't poisonous, I discovered, so, secret, I wiggled one secure behind

my back, in my overalls like a dove in a shooting vest.
By the ditch and cold sand water, I found Reeder's
Schlitz metal stripe beer can. I filled the bottom with dried pebbles

and seeds that would make it sound just like a Rattler. Reeder's
truck stopped. He called us to, "Jump bed." We were going
to move fields. I pulled the snake. I got set to join

the "God's of Hoeing," club, get old man Reeder himself.
I tailed the snake in my overalls and threw him just
at the heel of Reeder and shook the Schlitz can.

Reeder jerked, drew his pistol. "Goddammit!" Shot
the snake five times. Then, turned to me, eyes
wide as a coffee saucer, pistol barrel at my face.
The only sound was the water pump half a mile away.
I dropped to the sand crying, face as low as I could bury it.
His gun hand was shaking. "Don't need that again! Hear me!"

"You boys remember my son trying to get that rabbit out
of that irrigation pipe?" He pointed his gun down the road,
fired one frustrated shot at the vanishing point. "Trying

to get a new born rabbit out of its throat, struck
the highline wire?" "I'm sorry," I offered trying to cover all
my wrong doings. "Sorry don't set the table." The rest of the day

I chopped and pulled white-weeds, their thorns all the way
to their roots. Their toes held the soil, clinging, desperate,
battling with the new green bolls of cotton readying themselves for harvest.

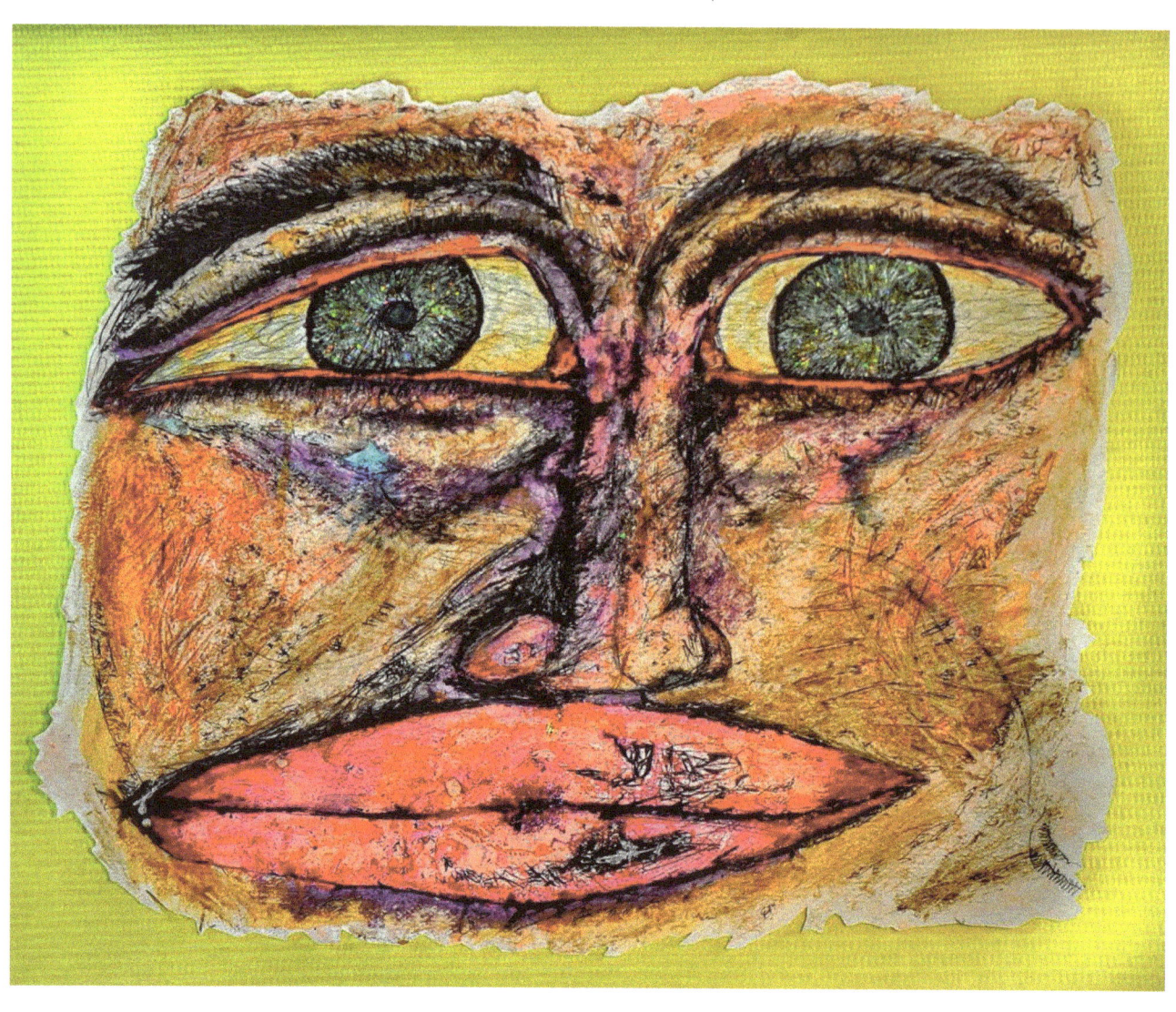

Watching the KKK Rally in Sulfur Springs, Texas

I didn't plan it. I didn't even know it was going
to happen. I just had stopped on the way
to Riley Springs to see Roy Acuff and to get a coffee,
local shop, on the square. I noticed it was
eerily vacant outside, but bustling inside the shop.

I ordered coffee and eggs, over medium, grits, sausage,
buttered toast and tomato juice, two lemon wedges.

"Rally starts anytime now." A man at the counter
offered. Then, I saw why everyone was inside packed
together. They were avoiding *being* outside. I watched
in disbelief as a KKK parade rounded the corner.
I physically jumped, the disgust churned
in my stomach and I lost my appetite. No one spoke.

It passed as soon as it had started. I needed
someone to settle my soul. The same man at the counter spoke.

"They sure are some stupid sonsofbitches.
Don't know why they even bother wearing them robes;
Everyone of 'ems dog's walking right beside 'em."

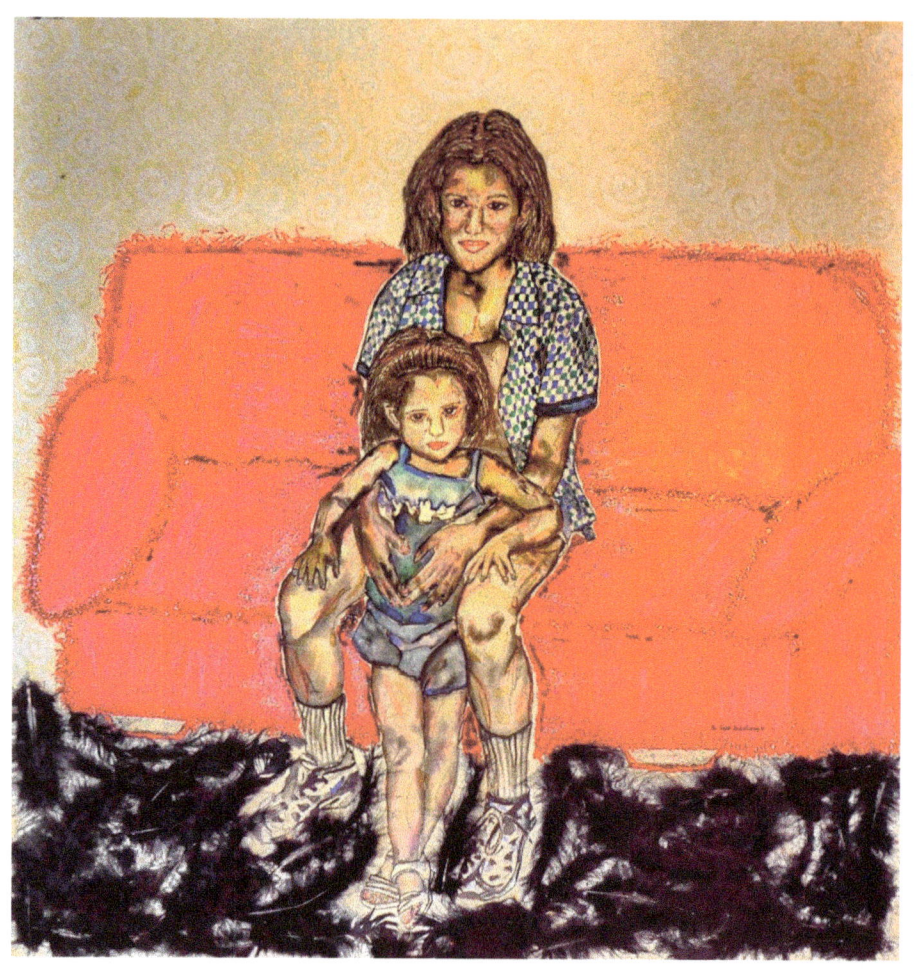

What Does the Cuckoo Do Inside Her Clock?

My first day on the job, I stood at the door,
nose against the door, testing the hinges, ready
to explode like a cacophonic steam whistle gone mad.
After awhile, it got too easy, armchair, cheese puffs, following
the simple rule: be on time; be constant.
They pull the pine cones tight to listen to me. Pulling
the chain gives me life, like a fix. Pulling.
I am their little God for those few seconds.
It's a real job being a Cuckoo.

I checked my daughter into rehab today, again; I know
the routine now. A lot of questions and honesty, followed
by lies and loud voices falsely vowing honesty. The feeling that
her lost journey is my fault, the open sea swallowing
her innocent sparkle green, the emptiness of witnessing
her become that which she has consumed.

In the movies, crazy looks pretty God
damned sweet, doesn't it? When it's
your little *Girl Interrupted*, it's not at all. At all.

Where did her glowing moon and stars go from her
fifth birthday ceiling surprise? You can't see the stars
when you're blinded by the darkness. Well, I un-nailed *my* feet from

the clock's thrust board, today, I took a leap out of this clock,
swan dived into the pool of humanity and responsibility
and encouraged her in, "When you're drowning,
the first thing to try is simply stand up. You might be in
water more shallow than you think. You might be able to," I begged.

She answered, "I don't want to stand up and I know how to swim, Daddy.
I just can't find the shore."   We hug.

Then, she let go—because it was time to go mark the hour.

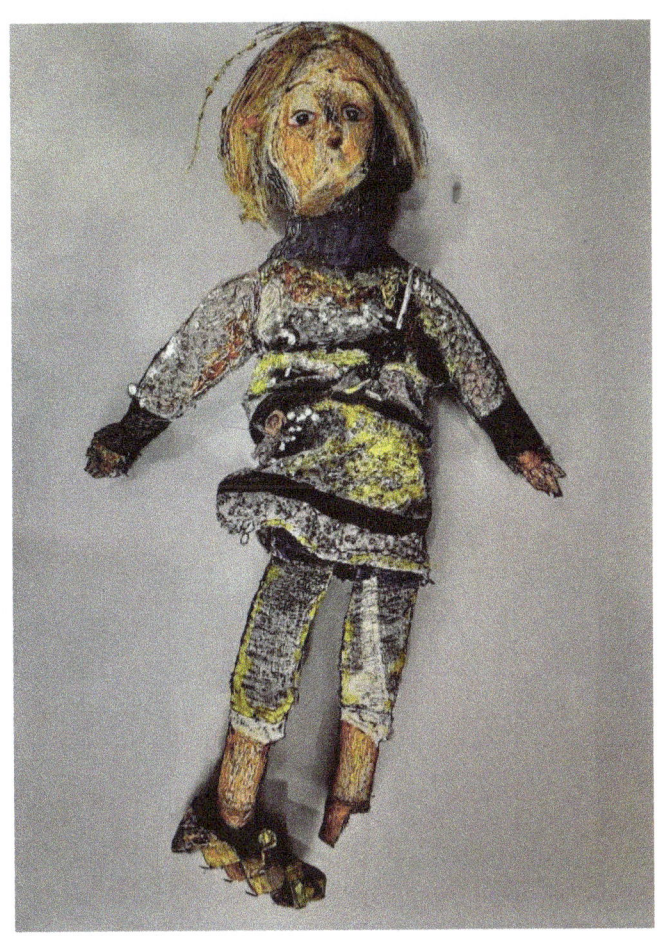

Eulogy: Why Ericka Hated Squirrels
For my neighbor who died of brain cancer

Perhaps Erika hated squirrels because they were
a mirror of her soul; we tend to desire
to destroy that which reflects us too faithfully.

Remember, Winston Churchill burned
the completed commissioned portrait
of himself. *It reflected him too faithfully.*

Suppose one were to strategically place cactus around
Erika's goal, like she did the squirrels, or glass in shards, or fencing,
or place that prize dangling, full of visible, precious
seeds just out of reach. Would Erika give up, or only see
it as a challenge? I suspect we would find her hanging
upside down from the chain, her cheeks chocked full of seeds.

She wanted life to be fair, a challenge
no doubt, but *fair*, like the chess match she played
with her squirrels in the backyard. She even told me
near the end that she, "Could not have
cancer;" she had done, "Nothing to deserve it."

Darcy and I found Erika's long body curled fetal on the kitchen floor
her silent mouth working like a fish out of water, I witnessed
"our squirrel"—our protector of the neighborhood, our one
who posted the night movements of the Coyote mother
leading her babies though our dark streets, our one who installed
the flood light as bright as God's front porch flooding
through our bedroom window every night, our neighborhood
guardian helpless in an unmoving body and I felt
as though our squirrel had been snared.

Darcy covered her to warm her. We were afraid
to move her, so we sat on the floor beside her.
We rubbed her legs and arms until the nurse arrived.
At one point, I even told her, "I Love You,"
as a sort of collective from us all,

almost like one says words alone
to a night sky expecting no response.
To our surprise, in full, clear, solid voice she replied,
"'I love you, too." Just ask Darcy and the floor and the blanket.

They heard.

Snared, entangled, our "squirrel" was still feverishly rebuilding her
jigsaw self, still trying to figure a way over that cactus to the golden
seeds dangling just out of reach above her tall figure, forever clad
in white overalls, waiting for her next tea party and her nemesis squirrels'
next move. Her final game she played was a wonderful, beautiful, graceful,
dignified checkmate; not a game lost, but a game transcended
beyond our understanding. But certainly, those searching squirrels
in her backyard standing on their hind legs, sniffing the air for
something, somehow knew they had lost their own reflection.

Bustie Girl and Charlie Pyewacket

My wife teaches Early Childhood Development—God
bless her soul. The Principal, a single
woman who can't figure out why
she's single, insisted the classrooms get pets.

The first pet was a Gecko who basically sat on his
heated rock mysteriously making all the live crickets
disappear at night. Next, were the fish who methodically, up
the food chain, ate each other, leaving one, lone, boring Sucker Fish—
Peter Plecostomus—who was addicted to the bubble castle with
the opening and closing treasure chest.

After came the Guinea Pig—Charlie Pyewacket. The kids had
found their love pet: they took him to recess; they let him play
in the outdoor lettuce patch; they brought him to reading circle;
they learned to get him to make his "O, O, O," British, "Hello,"
when they entered the room. Time Passed.

At Christmas break the "Special Needs" teacher needed to store
her Guinea pig with someone so she could get a divorce and get happy.
School pets don't go home or back to the school zoo; once they're in,
they're in. So the kids double-wided the trailer cage and put in
two igloos: Blue—boy: Pink— girl. Seemingly, overnight, they gave
Birth— "Immaculately," [it was explained]— on the very day of open house.
It was a "True Miracle." After general assembly, the children rushed
to show their, "Baby Jesus," to their parents.

The cage was red and wet. "A rat must have gotten
into this cage," one parent suggested. Another began
to try to shield the eyes of all the children running back and forth.

Sometimes in a double-wide cage, it's difficult raising children.
Sometimes fathers eat their newborns. Some say because
of displaced aggression, some say the fetus was abnormal.
Some say it's just out of plain meanness and a need for attention.

Still, that's science. That's why Jr. High is important. That's where
we learn how to live in-or-out of our cages, becoming animal or human.
Or, if you are really lucky and get a really good teacher—a bit of both.

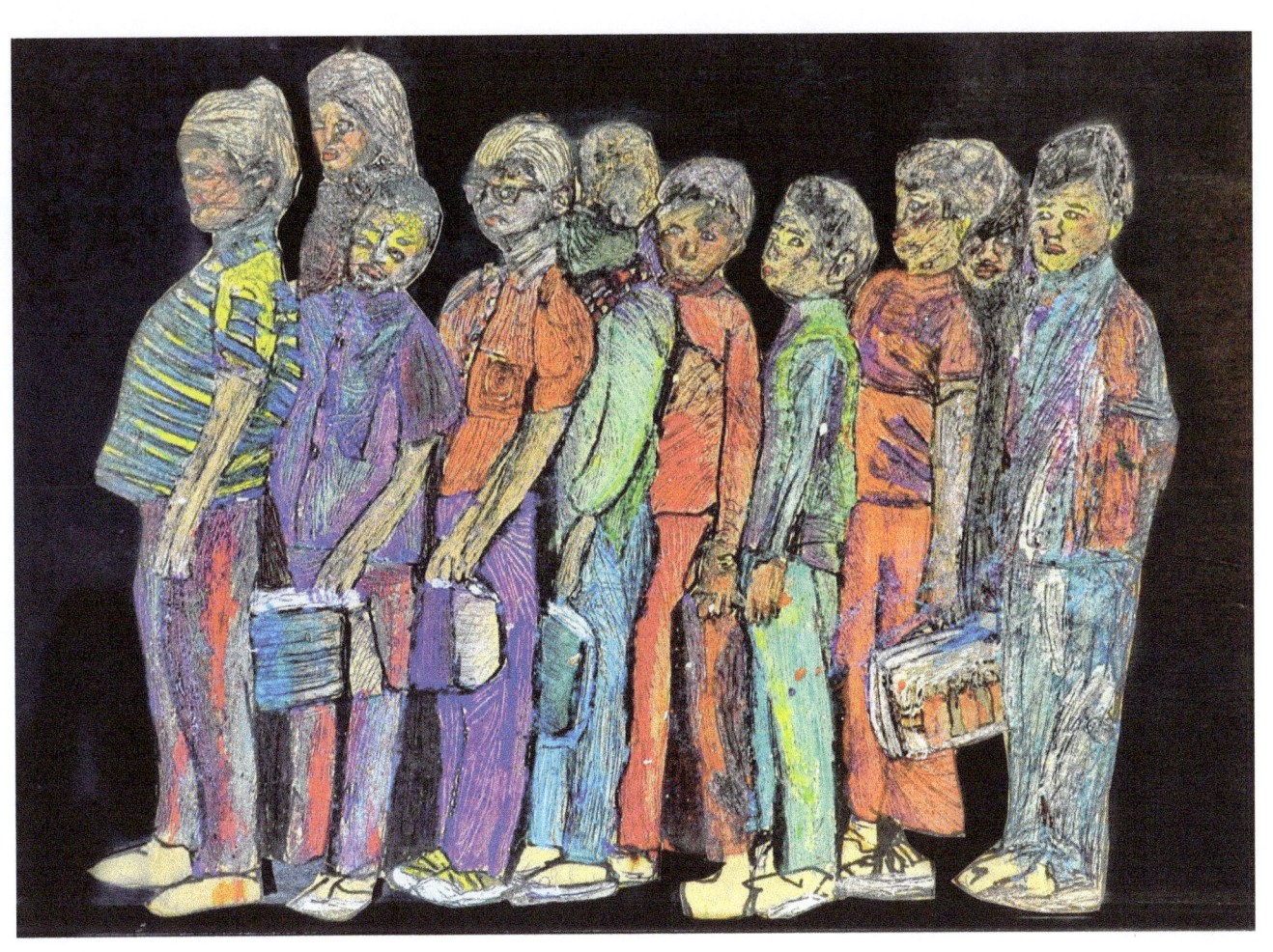

Ignacho's House Burning Down

Just before seven AM, Ignacho's house is burning down,
my next door neighbor. This is real. Trucks. Smoke.
Steam. His wife dropped in the yard where candy-red
sirens took her down the street, wherever screaming
sirens take you with their Fire Stix heads, the Doppler
Effect bending the night's noise in circles around
the tornados of fire and mist-white water and blue smoke.

He came out, only in his underwear: Ignaciao, like an Aztec God,
bronze skin defiant against the yellow, orange-red rising, melting
his home. His wedding pictures burn, his school picture of her
in 3rd grade when she was still Leticia Quezada at Cactus Elementary,
the four one-hundred dollar bills no one knew about in the fake
outlet box he was saving for her dishwasher, to be her
thirty-fifth anniversary gift. And the guitar he always meant
to learn to play he got for his Jr. High graduation.

In one hour, I stand with him watching the Totem Pole of his
ancestry, generations standing on each other's shoulders, on fire.
A man's history, solid and firm and sure, burnt to a boney carcass.

Fire is one of nature's cleaners that doesn't pick or choose;
it cleans in seconds. We stitch our eyes to sleep each night in Texas,
thinking fires, "Only happen in California and Colorado."

One sweep of a giant on the unsuspecting with an indifferent broom.

I try to comfort him, not with words—there are times to shut up—
but with a simple arm around his shoulder. Ignacio is the calendar
and clock in our neighborhood. I've never set an alarm. I just wait for
his truck to start. I've never seen him miss a day because he hasn't.

He showed me his hands one Sunday, raw and bleeding,
from Jack-Hammering a foundation, said he should have
taken his socks off to use as gloves; he added, "Just wasn't thinking."
Then, he gave me an iced Corona and a lime. He rubbed
his lime into his wounds and smile-grimaced, then rubbed in the salt.

"Ready for tomorrow; have to start rebuilding tomorrow—after work."

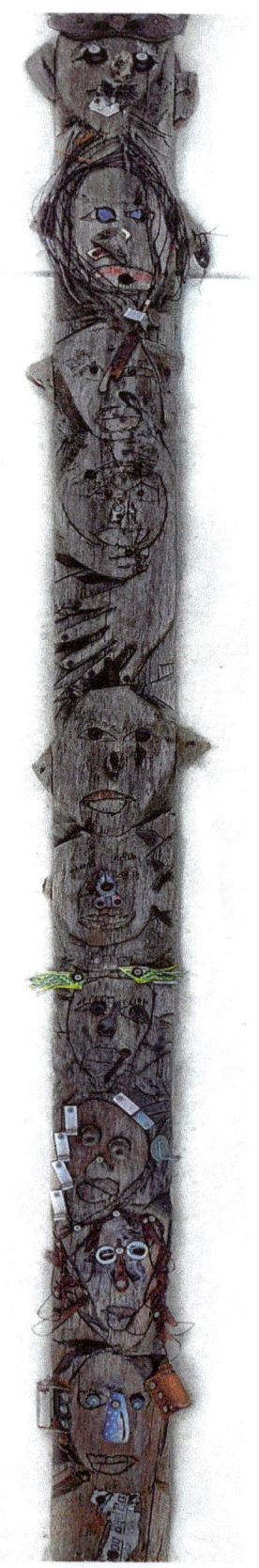

Notes from a Conversation: "How to Bet a Horse Race" According to Jim Jenkins [Live Stock Judge]

GENERALLY
- *Never* bet a LONG SHOT as A SHOW ticket.
- *Never* bet a BEST BET as A WINNING ticket.
- Both are ninety percent to lose or pay 20 cents on every ten

Only bet PLACE tickets after the following:
First—Look for a horse that has won something

Second—Track the horse's past; if they are going UP
in distance, don't bet them. For example, from a mile
race to a mile-and-a-quarter from their previous.

Third—if the horse is going down in distance, do
bet the horse IF not too sweaty [WARSHEET
is the term; already beat, meaning the trainer doesn't think
the horse has a chance or they wouldn't have,
"shot him up." Most times pisses the horse off,
but trainers do it. *Still, if you were the trainer?*
However, they usually loose [82%]. A horse being
shot up sweats just like a junkie.

Fourth—After tracking down [watching the first set
and second set of lanes to see which is favoring
that day] Only bet horses in the 1-10 to 9-20 section,
but only after also considering (1) if they are sweating [NO]
(2) are they going below a distance they have WON
before or have WON at that distance before
(3) Watch the horses before the race [Do they look
like a "good woman"/ "good man" or a
"whore"/"fucker-dog man person?" Good
women are alert, hoofs not dragging, smart,
horny, ready to run/reliable men are alert,
receptive, playful, responsible and alert to the Jockey.
They are ready to play and run, not looking
to get it over with—just like humans.]—Jim's words.

Fifth—Both horses male or female know
they are going back to a stall and how

they are treated; perpetual losing
horses are not happy. Watch for slow
hooves on the final walk around.

Sixth—After all that, if you can get your bet to two
horses, why not bet a Box Quinella and BOTH to place.

Lastly—Look at Jockey's past, with that horse,
at that distance, and if any lanes have been
suspiciously well. P.S. if you have done
your homework, why not bet the Daily Double
for two bucks. "Hope this helps you out."

P.S.S. NEVER bet on a name, a lane simply
because it is your favorite number, or the
horse that shits last. Never bet a best bet.

"Also, the reason I always honk at you and your
wife when I see you running together is because your
hooves are never draggin'. Love Ya'. Good Luck."

Makers of the Earth

After church my father sent me to the backyard
before the Pot Roast was done to kill the ants. I used
charcoal lighter fluid. Anytime I got to start
a fire as a kid was pretty cool. He had preached
on Adam and Eve that morning and I kept thinking
about Staci Odell's lips wrapped around that red
apple and the fire in front of me burning. I decided
I would have followed her, too, instead of "tending"
that garden naming animals, and, that word
"tending" sounded kinda like free-labor work to me.
My mother, Native American, came into the yard, she
was horrified—at the fire, I thought. She lifted
me up by one arm, spanking with the other at
the same time. "Why are you killing the makers
of the earth?" I was tremendously confused.

That night, I leaped faith, and reasoned it out. I know
from experience, all the ants don't die—no matter
how much you burn them or poison them or stomp
them—they just pop-up healthier and pissed-off
in the neighbor's yard and wait for you to ignore
them, and then, they just sneak back in silently.
Kinda like Adam and Eve. Kicked out, they left
the garden, had some kids that went all ape-shit
crazy over some vegetable sacrifice, one even killed
the other, and then that huge ass flood, and *then*
they got whacked out of the sky for building
a skyscraper, all in like seven pages.
Just like the ants, one yard after another.

It seems like an eternity that we've have been
trying to get back into our father's yard,
building stuff, trying new places, just being
how we were built, staying alive, waiting
patiently like the ants, until we can
tunnel in, or go over the gate, or climb
the fence, or wait for him to leave
the door open to check his fly or something,
but, it'll happen. Can't kill things meant to live.

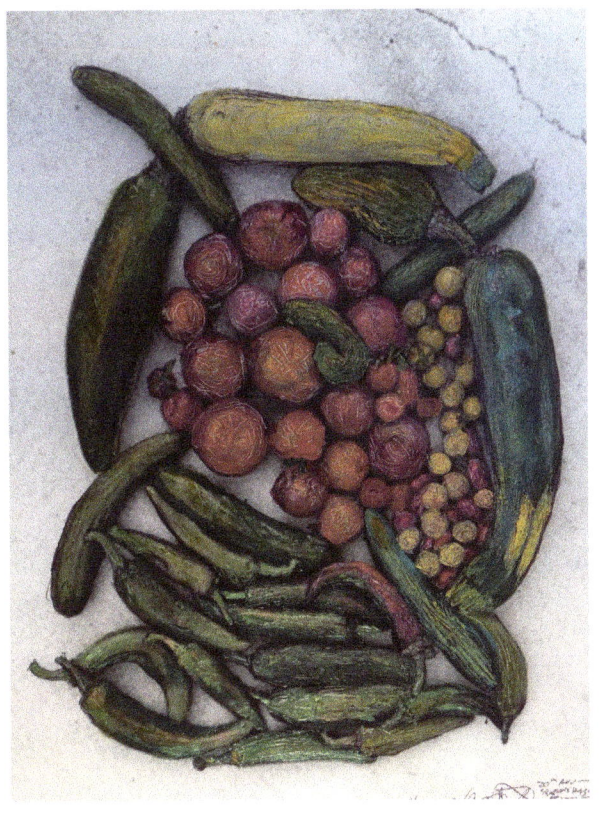

David's Father

He got up for the third time, Thanksgiving Eve,
just like he did every night to pee-again. Old man stuff;
but this time his step was stuttered by a misfire, a heart attack.

Most of us—when we fall—catch ourselves,
at least a bit, but a heart attack drops you flat.

I'm convinced his six- foot-three frame hitting
that flat floor may have just restarted
his heart's hiccup; his nose inside his slippers

he had never worn. Lorraine called.
The paramedics came. They took him
to the hospital, leaving us all open-mouthed
silent three hours later around the Thanksgiving Table.

His two grandsons, eight and six, knew something
was wrong—but we don't tell children the truth, do we?

Everyone talked me into taking them to the movie. Sometimes
you just do stuff because you don't know what to do, so I agreed.

We went to *Toy Story III*, the one with the really mean
Care Bear and "Thank God" *the* claw came out of the sky
near the end, directed by the aliens—Deus Ex Machina—
to save the whole bunch while Care Bear got strapped
to the front of a garbage truck grill, forever facing reality.

It killed time and we went outside after. Outside
always seems surreal after a movie, like it's not
the real world. Out here, the story is an already
started film, characters strewn all over, not directed
by *the* claw, plucking goodness from danger just in time.

We decided to walk around. They didn't want
to go back to, "that house stuff silence" either. We found

a fountain. The chlorinated coins reflected the blue sky.
Branson looked at me and asked why there was money
in the fountain. "People throw coins in and make a wish."

He stayed silent for almost a minute.

"Can I take one out?" I followed his twisting thought down
the rabbit hole. I held his socks and shoes as he tipped

his toes, stepped into the unknown reason of why
we do the things we do to gather that which,
we do not know why we need to do it, but we do.

Bill Hall's Dog

When my cousin Bill Hall killed himself,
he had thought most of it through, left
a pretty good note for everyone and a few
knickknack objects easy enough to distribute, but

he also left Butch. That's when we knew
something was bad enough and stopped judging.

When a dog can't fix something,
something is terribly wrong.

The family matriarch, cousin Diane, took it upon
herself to take Butch. Butch was a Weenie Dog.
Butch lived with Diane and her dog, Rusty,
until Butch's death of natural causes—whatever
that is. She opened a bottle of Scotch that night.
She has money, so a "good bottle," and decided
she would go bury Butch by Bill Hall.

"Diane, I can't let you dig Bill up," the graveyard manager
said as he approached her; she had a shovel.
"I ain't digging him up. I'm burying him."
She pointed. Butch was in a scotch box several
feet away. "Not supposed to let you do that either."

"Dead don't have no rules. You gonna help
me or am I going to hit you with this shovel."

He took the shovel and a slug of the Scotch. He
dug a very square, perfect hole. They took
another slug, poured one for Bill Hall in
a shot glass Diane brought and some water
in Butch's bowl she brought and left it
on the headstone and covered Butch up.

"He's where he needs to be now." "I got two
squares of nice Bermuda I'll put over him
before sunrise—if you'll leave the rest of that."

She gave Conrad the rest of the bottle after one
final slug and then she drove home, her
head against the steering wheel. "Goddammit!"
She honked her horn three times when

she crossed the railroad tracks and put
herself to bed and waited for the sun
to rise, as it always does for some reason,
like nothing ever even happened: the maid
of light that sweeps away the dark each morning.

For some reason that seems right, or the real
world would just be too much to bear.
New, clean, days are important.

Otherwise it would make sense just to shoot yourself.

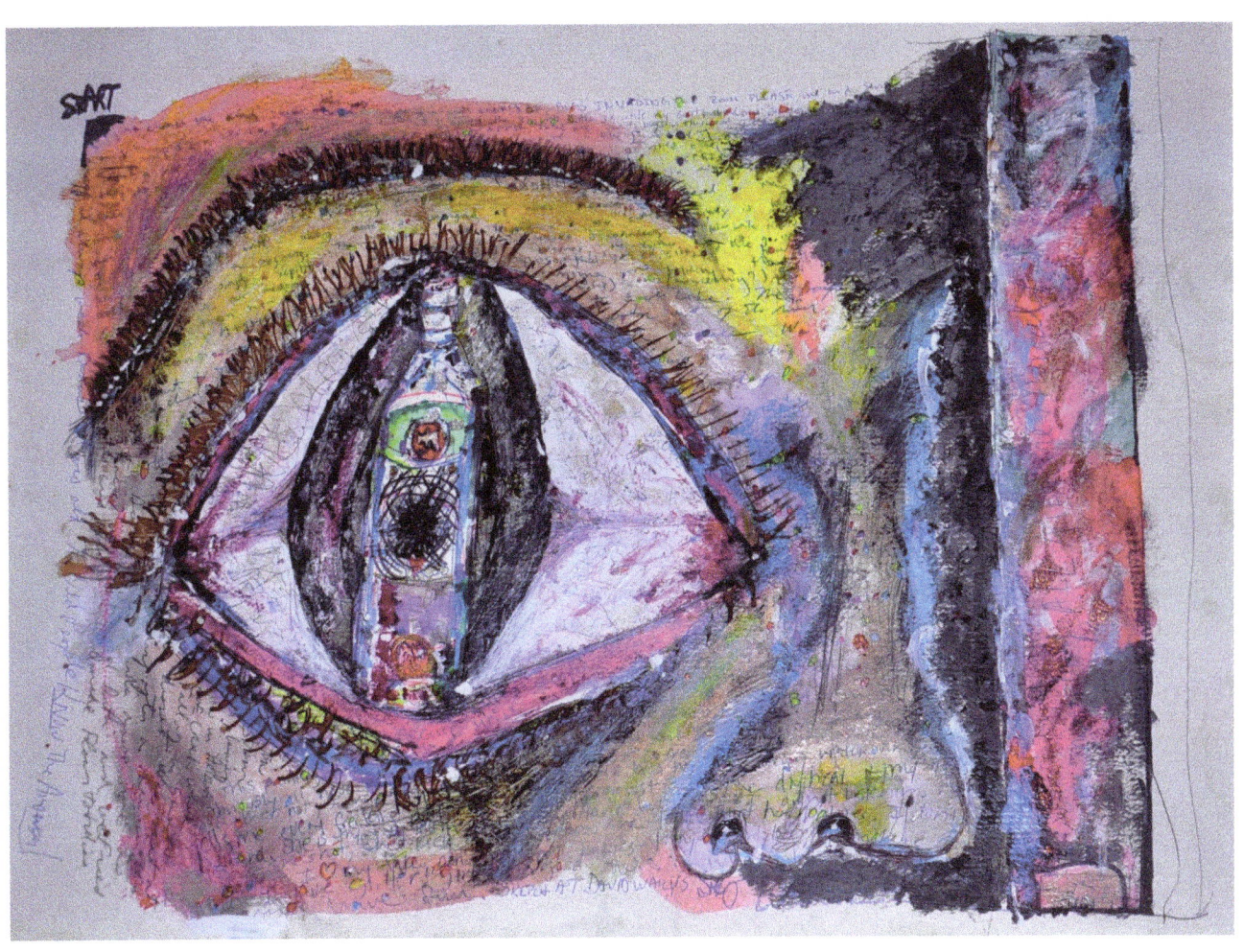

Getting Old at Sam's Club

Get the card that lets you in before regular hours, before
all the people who *have* to shop can come in. That way
you also get the small pleasure of getting to go "in"
the "out" door, like I imagine riding first class
on a plane must feel. Buy their eggs, their cheese,
their frozen Salmon blackens well, the tenderloin
is decent, Dunkin Donut coffee, maybe even
that new big screen TV to watch Wheel of Fortune
or the same news story over and over with
the skin disease commercials in between.

But, above all, get a hot dog and a drink for $1.62:
a Nathan's Frank, steamed bun, Heinz mustard,
and, if you ask, an individual sauerkraut packet
to make a damn good kraut dog. You can get
as much or as little ice as you want. You can refill
your drink when you want and as many times
as you want and don't have to wait for someone
to ask if you want your drink refilled incorrectly.
You can use as many napkins as you want. You can
also watch everyone wrestle their single piece
of pizza while inwardly smiling, knowing
the hot dog was the obvious best choice.

Also, most old people clean up after themselves.

Then, roam around and speculate if you can really
eat 152 assorted Snickers, 3 Musketeers, and Almond
Joys; then, take them back out of your basket. You
can even go down the "Man" aisle and look
at tools and generators and oil and work benches
and touch them and remember you don't have
to do any of that shit anymore because you make
enough money to pay someone else to crawl under
your car, unscrew one screw, drain your oil—and it's worth it.

Then, you can check yourself out if you're
a "Do-It-Your-Selfer," or have the young college
girl check you out who *has* to be nice to you.

And when you leave, the guy at the door to check your
criminal history by marking your receipt—it's usually
a guy—and he will act like he's, "Really glad
you came," and that, "It's a pity that you are leaving."

Then, you can look for your car in the parking lot because
you forgot where you parked, and, because you don't really
have any place else to go until Costco opens, it doesn't matter.

I mean, it's open if you have the upgraded card, but no
reason to have two upgraded cards. That wouldn't make
a bit of sense; not when you're old at Sams.

My Eye Exam from the Guy at Whole Foods

When you wear glasses and you break the only pair
you have, you have to wear your prescription sunglasses.
It's not comfortable and terribly inconvenient,
but seeing is kind of important.

I was hit in the eye with a baseball at age
six; I'm blind in my right eye, except for light.
That is to say, that's why I was wearing my prescription
sunglasses to go into the grocery store. I don't

normally frequent Whole Foods either, but when
I discovered a grocery store that allows me
to drink a beer while I'm shopping—I went all in.

At the bar I asked the 'tender to put my beer
in a "flat bottom cup;" the small beers come
in a stemmed glass. It doesn't "ride" well
in the cart. I had once before spilled my shopping motivation.

The guy next to me felt the obligation to make an assumption,
"Wearing *sunglasses* in a supermarket, *asking* for special beer glasses."

His sarcasm was as slow as the checkout line. He knew

I heard him; I ignored him. He continued;
I decided to see how long he would go.
At five minutes, I had the epiphany.

I have the ability, because of the eye injury, to cross
my right eye insanely, that is, without crossing the other.
It's a rather wonderfully disarming look.

He knew he was being offensive; the bartender was
getting a bit wiggly, too, so I crossed my one eye as
horrendously as possible. I took off
my glasses; then, as politely as possible, turned and asked
him which beer he might recommend. His face
fell, shifted, and he said, "Whichever, you pick.
I'll get us both one." He chose the highest alcohol content.

"I'm sorry; you are too kind." I replied. "No way can I take
that beer. I would be too embarrassed if I reached

for the glass that was not there, and for some reason,
it's extraordinarily dark in here. Still, I appreciate your kindness."

I put down a ten and instructed the barkeep to put
it toward his tab and went shopping, cross-eyed,
in my double darkness, just praying I don't come home
with two of everything, and taking his advice, reminding
myself that to see one thing clearly, I must always
focus, out of both eyes, on the vanishing point.

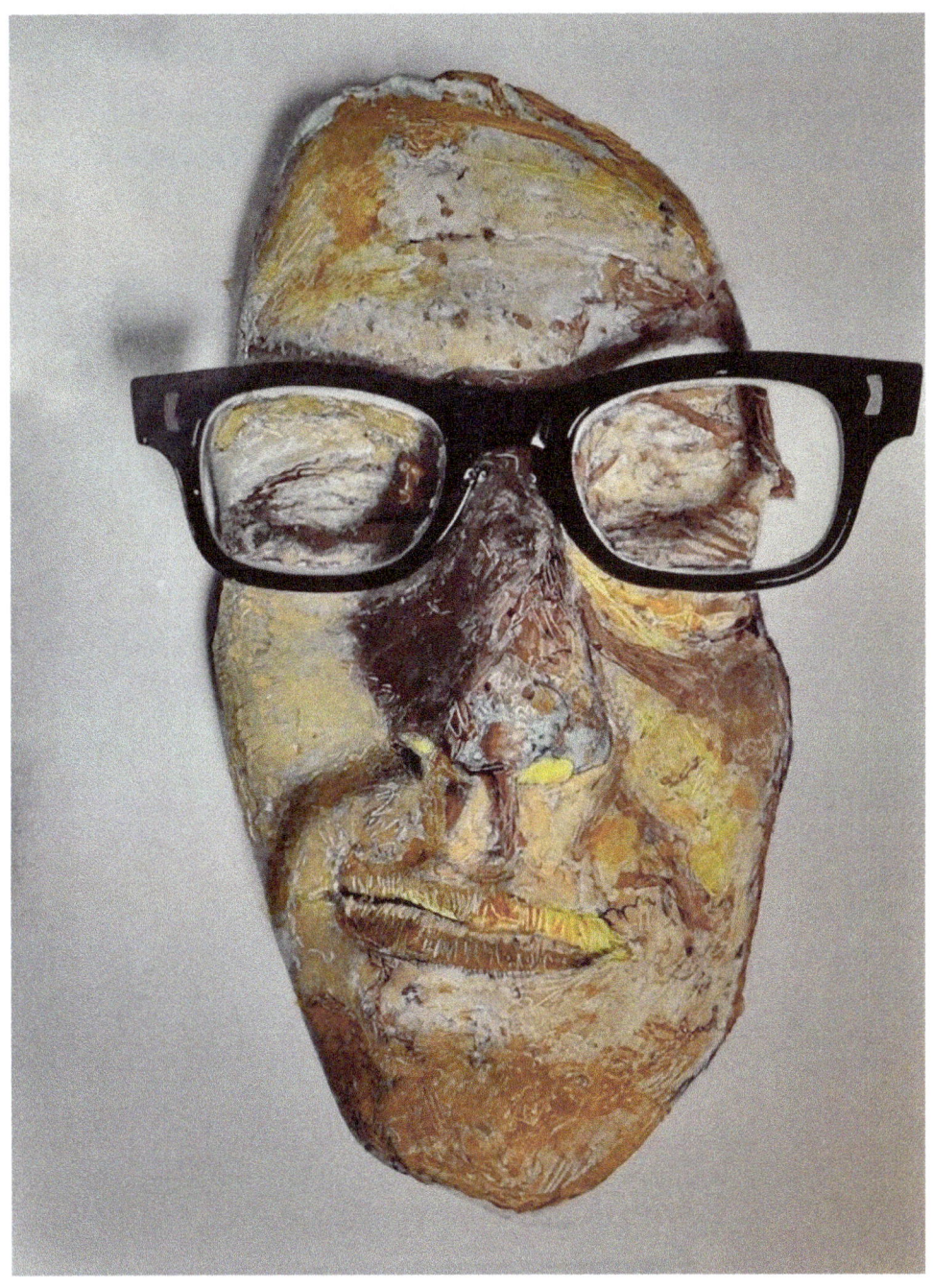

This One Round: Golfing Single

I enjoy golfing alone—sometimes. I can
work to make at least one true, pure par.

A goal. Nothing else matters for eighteen holes.
And I have eighteen holes to do it. Nothing else.

However, golfing single almost always gets you paired
with someone—so you don't hold the world captive,
a world in a hurry waiting for one. I've learned not
to talk at first, simply to see who I am playing.

They didn't curse on the first hole; I knew not to curse.
They didn't drink when the cart girl came by, so I waited
until I ended in the rough to make my cocktail I brought.

"Lula and Richard" had nice clubs, an older couple.
Both had gold shoes on and matching bags. They were
serious enough. She was very constant, almost always
in the fairway, one more to the green, and steady one or two putt.

Our conversation was, "Good shot," or, "You'll straighten
that out on the next hole." The husband didn't speak until
the back nine and asked me why I was limping. I explained
the surgery and how this was one of my first times out since.
He said he was a doctor and that he was proud of me.

Then, it happened. On seventeen—Lula found herself deep
in the rough, the high grass behind two trees. She tried hitting
over the trees, clipped one, and ended in the sand trap. She
cursed under her breath, then sand-chopped two. She started
crying. "You'll straighten it out next time," I tried.

"My son and his wife are getting a divorce. Twenty-two
years. Got the kids in college and . . . " "He doesn't want
to hear *all that*. For God's sake, we're on seventeen,"
Richard pushed his putter into the bag.

He wasn't angry, just firm. We golfed

eighteen; they both pared. I hit in the lake. Dropped
a ball and putted around like a kid at Putt Putt
ready to be done until I finally dropped it in the hole.

At the club house, he got out of the cart and went to the bathroom.

I took her hand for a second and patted her back. Our
eyes confirmed there was nothing to say. I got
my clubs, having parred five and twelve and fourteen
without cheating and went home to hug my wife.
I hugged her harder than usual without explanation.

I wanted to hug my one, good, pure thing I knew for sure.

"So, you got your par. That's a good day," she kissed me,
then returned to peel the orange in her left hand
leaving only the shells on the cabinet to dry.

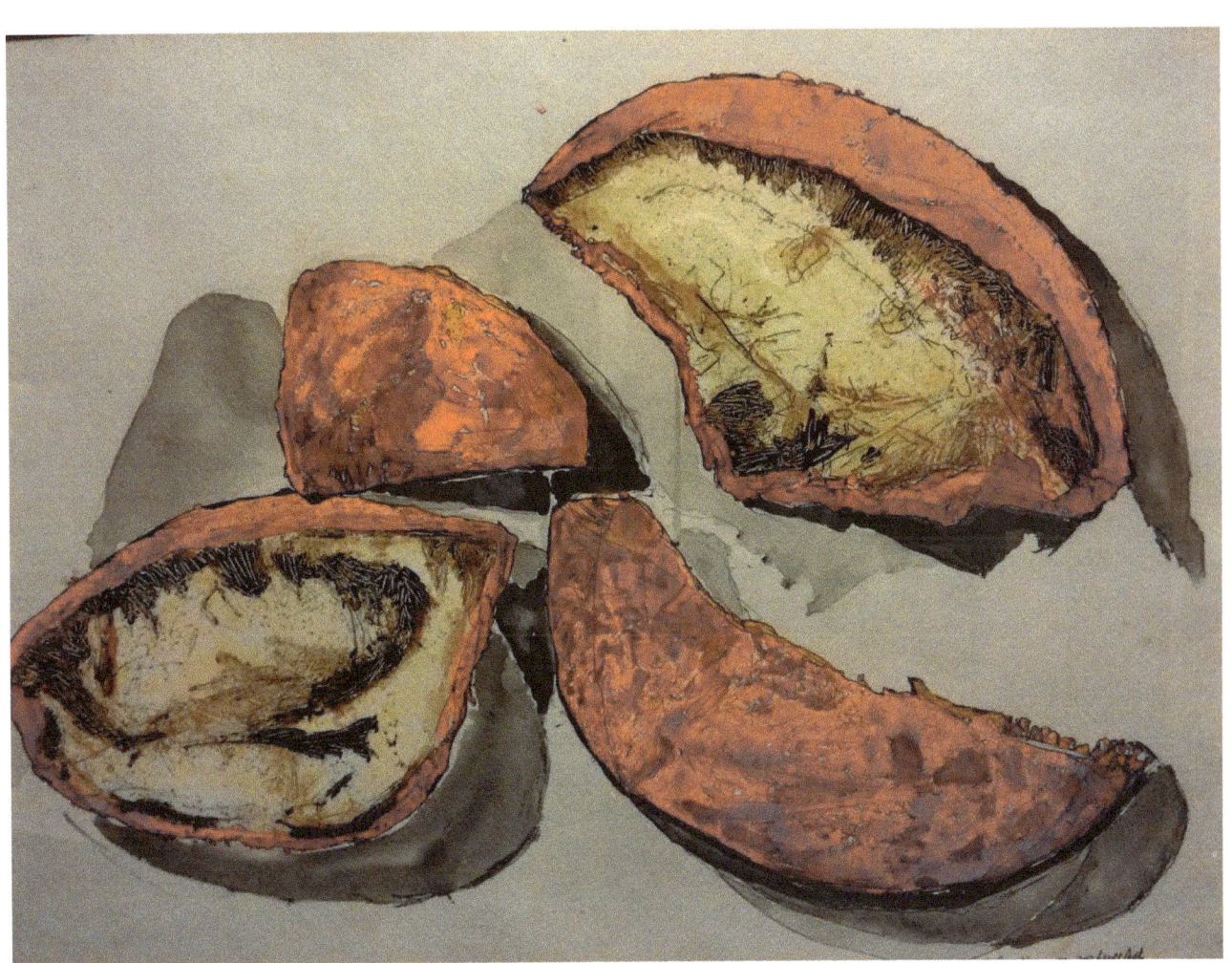

Mother and Beverly at the Alzheimer's Unit

Beverly stood at the door like a gatekeeper.
I watched her wind up, a clock ticking
up each face and voice as they pressed
the code to enter, an awareness of being
unaware. A year ago when she was brought in;
she had barely spoken—although she smiled
and laughed at the right time: her wires
had been cut from her phonograph needle
to her speaker. Exactly that simple.
She just needed to be rewired, rebooted.

I had seen her twice since she was admitted. Then,
her single repetitive phrase was, "Can I go
home now," like she was in timeout, being punished;
she had served her time in the corner, anxious to
return to the playground, having learned her lesson.

When we arrived, Dad went directly to misdirect
her husband; he never shuts up. My father is good
at knowing when to do what. As mother pushed
the last set of codes on the third locked
door, I told her. "Beverly is usually standing
right where the door opens. She will be right
there when it opens." I was just preparing
her. Tears. Mother, who had been
avoiding this moment for a year, witnessed
her reflection of that which she hopes
never to become. Even at eighty-three
they are beautiful women, happy, stand
the same, hands in a gracious giving
position in front, the same laugh. Hair
"just so" and clothes clean and pressed,
like Estelle, their mother, had taught
them "proper girls" should look.

Beverly, who had not spoken in over
a year, and recognized no one, even
her husband, broke into a cry, "Sister. Sister. Sister."

My mother, whom I have never seen cry—
except when her father died—cried. Tears
ran down her high cheek bones and her lips tightened.

She took Beverly by the hand and did
what she always does for most situations.

"Well nothing's going to get done just
standing around. Let's go on a walk,"
and they covered every inch of
every hall, "Sister," ringing out
over and over as if Beverly were introducing
Mother to all the lost who were found for
a brief moment between lunch and ice cream.

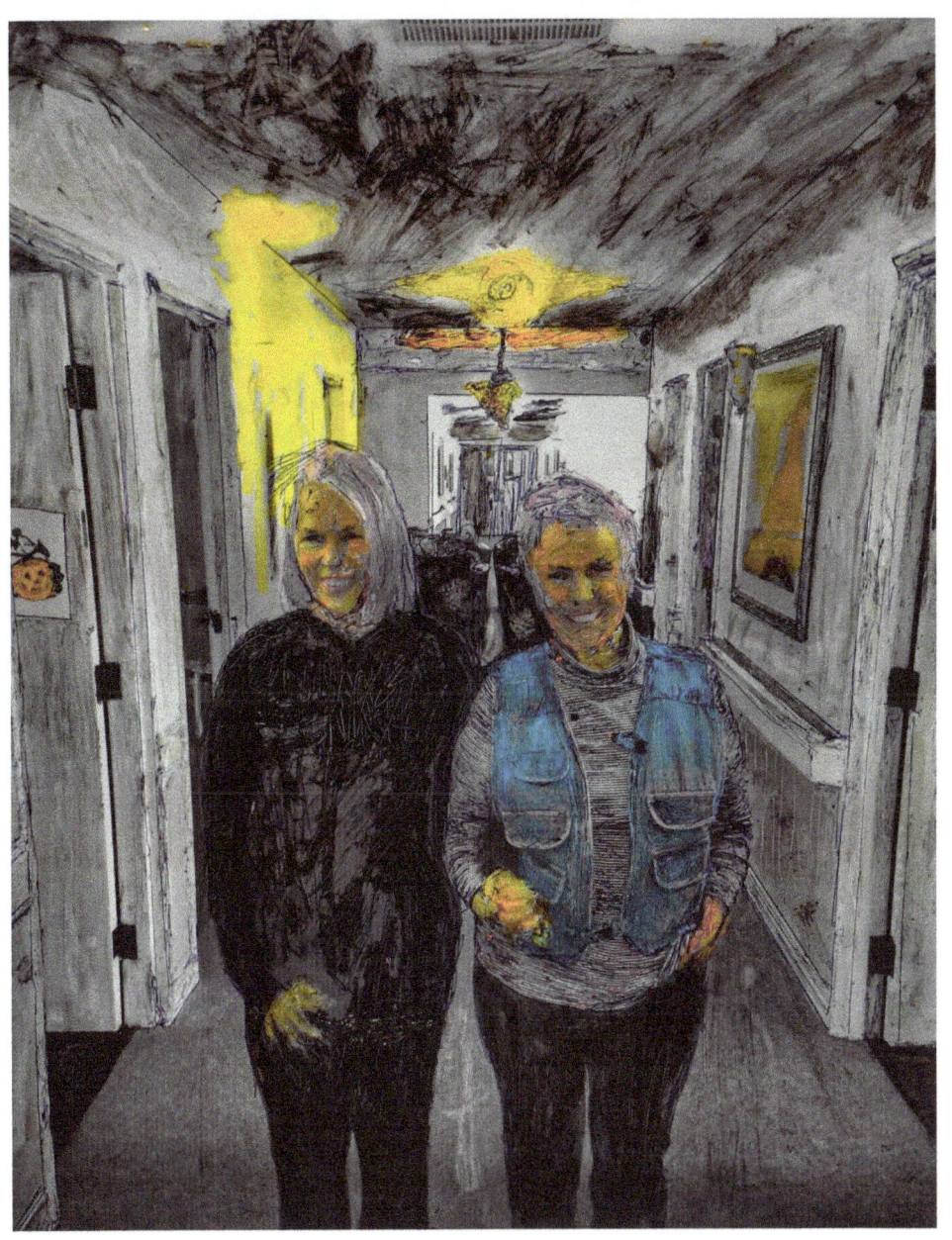

The Best Lawn on this Side of the Block

On the refrigerator weekly chore spinner,
I got "Dandelions"—this was a new one.
I was to take a kitchen knife or screwdriver into
the yard and "eradicate" the Dandelions—

I had to look up "eradicate."

Once down on my knees, I began to wonder
why my father hated them so much, or if
he was just starting to test us in one way
by making us do something stupid another.

I didn't question though. I got my tool
and picked one and blew it; I didn't realize
I was releasing a barrage of seeds to float
through the air to plant in new places at
the whim of the wind. Seeing me, my
father yelled, "Don't blow them. That
only spreads them and makes more. Eradicate!"

When he was watching, I would diligently screwdrive
the weeds out by the roots, careful not to spill
their tops; when he wasn't, I would carefully pull
each flower and blow it, spreading the seeds to curl their
tiny toes into the soil at the whim of their landing.

What did he hate about them? That they were
taller than the grass; that they were symmetric
and beautiful? What did he want, only to see
a conformed sea of green spreading with
no variance, no rifts in the current, no
plant standing more proudly or higher,
drastically distinct from the others?

Color

I parked myself, sitting crossed-legged in front
of the new color TV, nose close enough to touch
the screen, my mother swearing this new invention
was going to turn humanity, "Cross-Eyed." Then,

it happened. Dorothy stepped out of that house, opened
that door, and suddenly I was transported into "Oz,"
a scene as if Van Gogh, Monet, and Toulouse-
Lautrec all rolled themselves into a ball and then
exploded color and form into my black and white world.

Mother was right.

I was cross-eyed for months trying
to digest my new eyes, working both
at the same time, out of harmony, in
separate directions trying to see, trying
to understand how only *my world,* up
to that point was color.

The dark black on a uniform startlingly became
what it was: red rich blood. The ocean became
aquamarine. Snow became a new white: *snow white*.

Until then, the world across the screen was
black-and-white, two tones, contrast and focus.

The world went from a simple "yes" and "no,"
"right" and "wrong," to the visible spectrum
of colors somewhere over the rainbow.

My Stupid Watch

In First grade I left my new Christmas watch
on the playground on purpose. I got
a good spanking for that one. Mother
had saved Green Stamps all year for it.

But I had found I had a problem counting
things, like the 493 ants in the red ant bed behind
the backstop—give or take that one
with the stick somedays, somedays not. He always
conspicuously returned during count without it.

So I felt a comfort in getting rid of it, even with the spanking.

I had all alone tricked a machine
ticking for no reason about
a world it didn't even understand.

Time is fluid. Not tick-tock, start-stop.

When my wife bought me an I-Watch,
I couldn't bring myself to tell her
I can't wear handcuffs.
I wore it reluctantly.

Sometimes, someone else's feelings
are more important than your own.

Soon, I found it tracked my mileage, my exercise;
After a stake out, I found it even had an affair
going on with my phone. Then, it started telling
me what to do, to, "Stand up, to breathe,
that yesterday I was a *much* better person."
That next week I needed to work at not being
such a sloth. I even found its compliments
were laced with sarcasm. "You beat yesterday's
total before noon; today you are behind."
Which implied the next day, to feel good

about myself I really needed to have
my entire life done, and in order before 11 am.

I considered accidently swimming with it on and
drowning it, or accidentally backing over it with
the El Camino, but I had to find a way to beat it.

I turned it over all night like the possible
twin ant with the stick in a jar. I got it.

I dressed carefully for my walk the next day. I went
the exact same route, exact same time, and as I got
closer to "closing my ring" my smile widened.

I had purposely worn two black socks that did
not match. One subtle shift that only I knew
with every secret step; an ant with a magic stick.

When my wife asked, beaming, if I liked my new watch
I told her I loved it and I did. It allowed me disobedience
against time, my nemesis since grade school and playgrounds.

Atlas in a Lawn Chair

"It's your turn to check on Mom and Dad," my brother
reminded. When I arrived, Dad had started his 10 am
ritual; he had about forty cans lined up. Mom had
set each carefully down in a tight line, behind the back
right tire of the El Camino. He waved me into
the passenger seat, started the engine and put it into reverse
and backed slowly until each can was squashed, then
methodically, in drive, he forwarded back over them.

The church ladies brought him forty cans each morning.
They brought them for him to squash for the poor.

I held the trash bag as he pinched each one
with his "Miracle Grabber" claw extender
and he clinked each one in. Mom wrote down
the total, and waved from the porch. She
was clockwork sitting in her green and
white lawn aluminum lawn chair—She
waved I guess in case I hadn't seen her,
or just as an I'm still here, "Hello."

It was the same chair my father would sit
in after lunch in the garden with the hoe
and cut his twenty weeds within the diameter
of his circle center; a sun dial with a hoe, marking time.
Then, he would take his nap; his work was done.

After nap, mother put the chair by the grill,
water in an empty industrial gallon-sized
Jalapeno can to cover the applewood
chips he used to throw on the coals
to smoke the bone-in Ribeye.

After he woke he checked the weather and who
all got killed or died or pissed someone off
that day on the evening news, then got me,
to pull him out of his recliner, mother
put his Pajama bottoms on.

"It's good to see you, son," he hugged me
as he hobbled to bed. "It's good to see you too, Father."

We always call him Father.
He is our keeper of the globe, our
world firmly spinning as it should
on its axis, because he has our back.

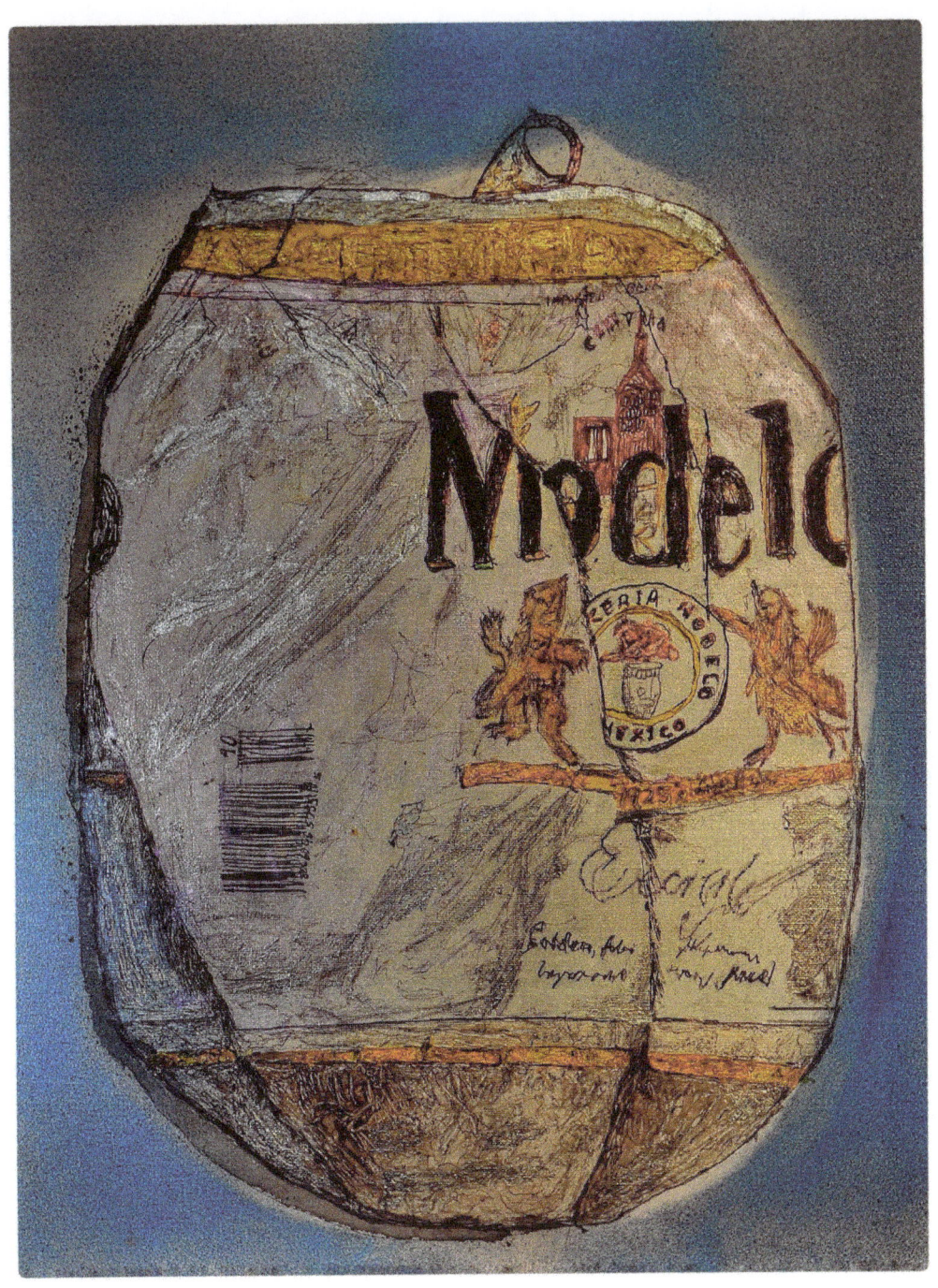

Chores

Don't need an alarm if you have chickens and the
sun. Today's a big day, important I do things right.
I keep the chickens in a school bus that my brother,
Roger, got from the auction. It don't run, but all
the windows close and the door. A safe roost.
We put 'em in at sun's eye closing. Well, I do.
Roger ain't able no more.
Live long enough and you'll understand.

I shoo 'em out at sun's first wink 'cause during
the night's when they churn up an egg.
Then, throw the feed so they get movin'. After a bit,
I check back in their favorite hay bales and insulation,
wherever I found 'em before, and gather.

The pigs slop second. Last night we made rounds by
the bread company and bought the three day olds they's
gonna throw out, total five dollars; they hold it for us.

Well, I did, Roger weren't able to get in the truck.
Live long enough and you'll understand.

Pizza place, D. Q., public school cafeteria, and then
mix in the corn. We feed 'em on palates so's we
can wash their mess down underneath where Roger
and I put wire mesh above the pit and the drain trough.

Pigs eat too fast so a lot of the corn don't digest. We got
to wash off the droppings, but the mesh catches the corn
so we can set it in the sun, feed it to 'em
again. It don't make them no never mind.

After, I take the greyhound down to hunt river rabbit
down by Black Creek. They's bigger than Cottontail,
smaller than Jack and tender as quail. Darndest
thing to see them two ears up like a periscope, those
back haunches purring the water with those pink-pawed
paddles. I get one. I get him back, skin him, and hang
the pelt in the barn, get the crock going and add a few
potatoes. I get an ice cold Co' Cola in a bottle
and go down to Roger's shed behind the house.

Roger's sittin' at the table facing away from me. He's my
brother so I give him a hand on the shoulder and put

the plate of rabbit and 'tatoes and Coke on the table
and the pistol down on the right side.

He pushes the plate away. I wait a minute and pull
it back; he pushes the plate back away and pulls the pistol,
best he can, in front of him, and barely able
to lift his arms, he points, shaking intolerable, at his head.

If you love a brother like you love any animal
and they's suffering beyond repair, you do what
makes sense. It let's the sun rise right the next day.

I put a towel between the barrel and Roger's
head and my hand on his shoulder, because that just
seemed right. Live long enough and you'll understand.

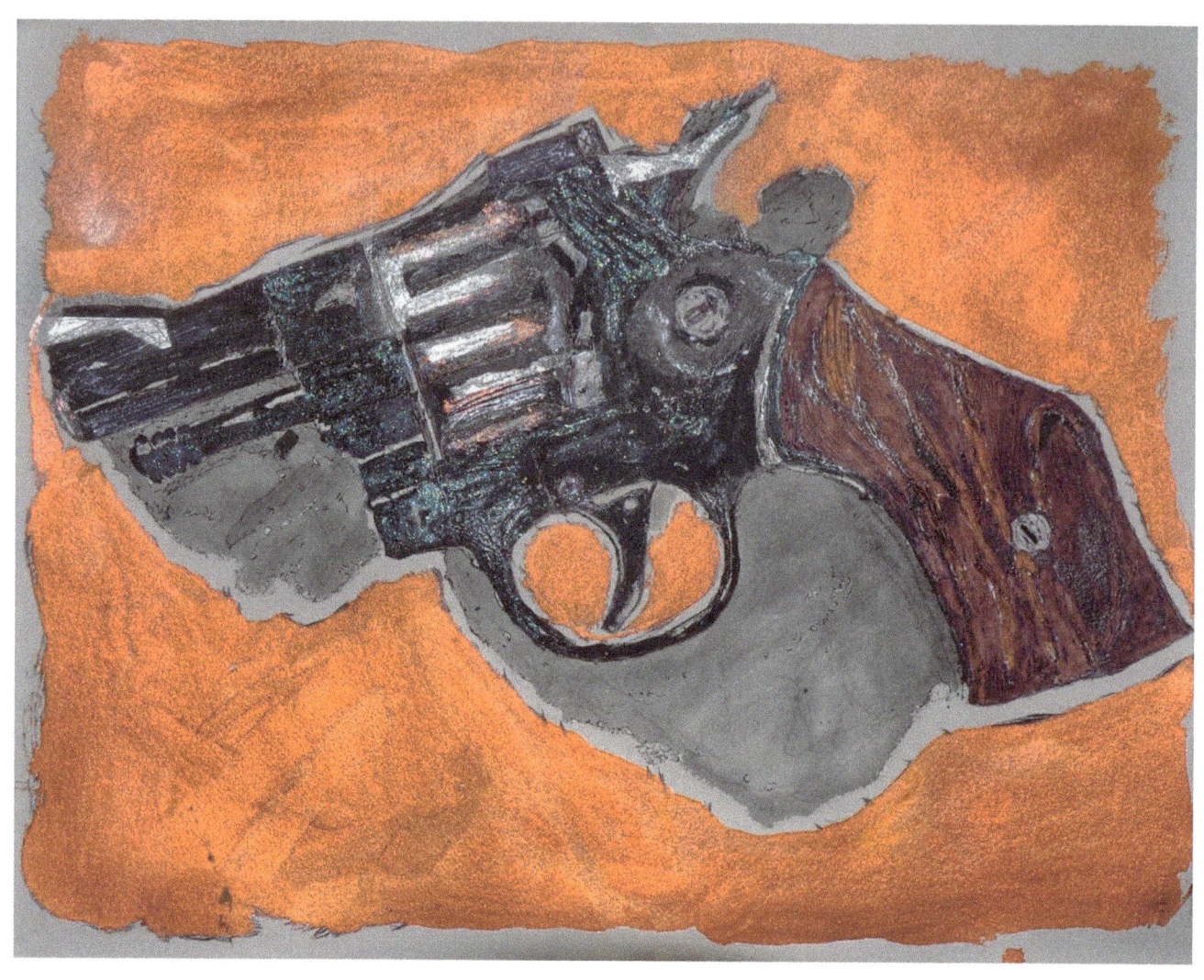

Becky Watches Big Tex Burn Down

I had the vats filled and up to heat
when I seen the smoke coming from
Big Tex's neck. Working Fletcher's Corndogs
as long as I have, I knew they's always doing
some darned new thing to update Tex
for people, but this seemed a bit much.

It was like when I cut my bangs for Billy
and got me that miniature skirt in August.

It was still me, but too much, too different.

Then, I looked closer and reevaluated.
This smell was a 'lectrical fire, 'lectric
wires burning. When his mouth blowed
out fire? Well, that's when I knew something
was for real wrong: no one want's, "Fire Breathin' Tex."

His shirt and britches went up like oily
corndog wax paper held over a propane flame.
People screamed, started running. One man throwed
his Root Beer on one of Tex's boots—feeble attempt.
At least he give something a give-go. Little babies
on the go round was pointing, little tears and screams
coming outa their baby mouths. Less than twenty minutes

Tex was a skeleton of rebar; his hands and part
of his face and boots was still recognizable—they's
made out of fiberglass. I know a good corndog girl's

not supposed to cry in public, but I wept. Most

don't know what a tough life Tex has had. He was
born a Santa Claus in Keren, 'bout thirty miles
over'nother town, before they bought him for
seventy-five dollars for here. They stripped
him of his Santa outfit, lost him a bit
of his weight and dressed him cowboy
and propped him up here at the State Fair of Texas.
Some say they even let Bill Brag live inside his boot so's
his movin' mouth could have a good Texas voice.
He could even ask people where's they's from and all
sorts or real life stuff; he was alive all right.

Must be a hell of a life getting to be a giant Santa
Claus and then Big Tex, just like all them damn Disney Kids
growin' up. Probably why he died so young;
just turned sixty this year. He always seemed happy.
Also, think of all that attention, *then* all that time off,
after, when there ain't no fair. That ain't fair to nobody
nohow; I say it must have been all that
time off. Devil's playground.

He was kind of like God, not Little Baby Jesus, Daddy
God, the overseer, the protector. He was a place
to meet where you knew where you were and
knew you were safe, and to see him burn up
in the time it takes to deep fry a couple
of corndogs—well, it's just beyond me.

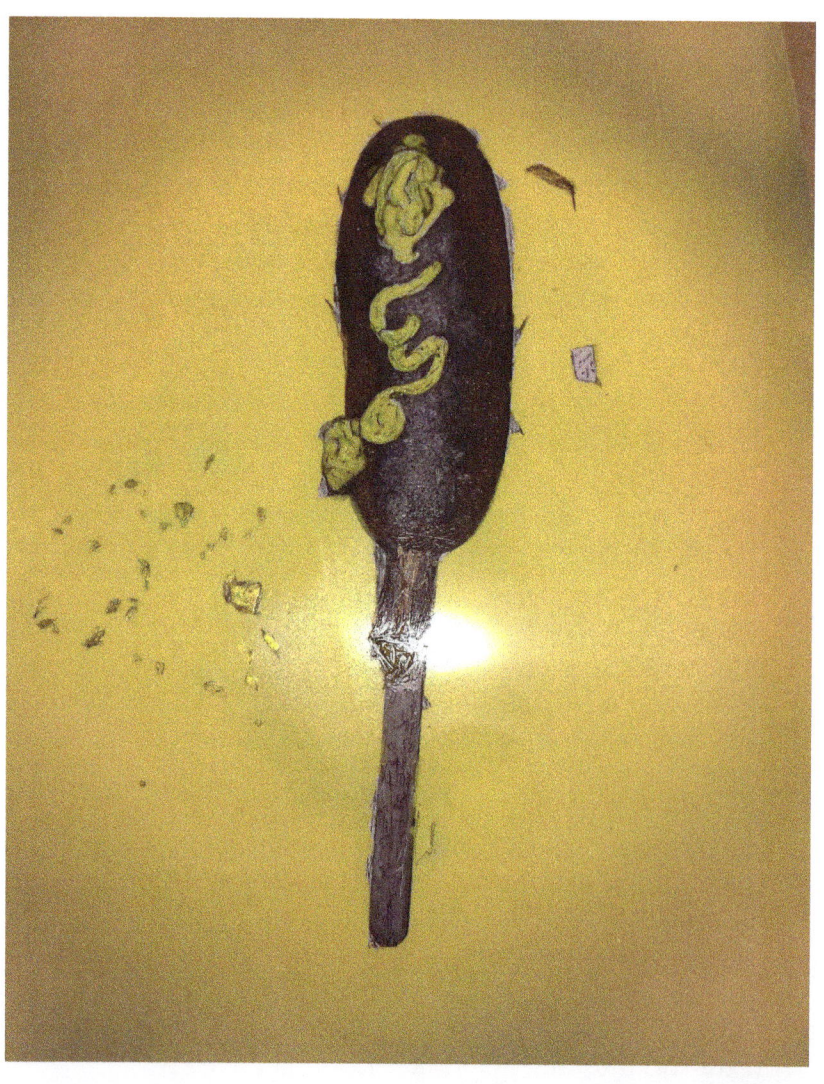

Going to the Dump in the City

In West Texas going to the dump is
a matter of driving out to where the Caliche
pit is that built the highway you drove out
there on and dump everything out.

There's no gatekeeper.

In the city, you have to go to the right
dump, the right zip code, and dump only approved
items, no chemicals, and somehow pass Janus,
the gatekeeper. God, she's a gruff
woman. Her half empty pack of American
Spirit cigarettes is always just behind the slide window.

I pull up to the, "stop-behind-the-white-line," line. Janus
moves her ashtray just behind the slide window
and tells me to back up because I was on the line.
I quickly digested this lady is going to find *something*.

So I just did it. Play along.

I backed up about half a foot. She closed the window.
No one was in front of me. About a minute later she opened
the window and waved me forward as if she had just
noticed I was there. "Don't have any chemicals in that
load do you?" ""No Mam," I sat up straight in my
bench seat —*a grown man scared of a dump lady.*

She repeated accusingly , squinting her eyes,
"If I go lookin' in there, I ain't gonna find any Chemicals?"
"No Ma'am'" "I see some metal." "Yes, Ma'am."

"*Are metals chemicals?*" I considered.

"Well, you got your current water bill." "Yes 'Mam."
She thrust out a yellow hard hat and an orange vest.
"Get out and put these on." Felt like I was at the doctor.
 I did and she inspected me and adjusted both,
pointed to a pile of metal, "That's where to put the metal."
Try to keep a neat stack. Then, you go by the fence
to the unloading barn. She pointed to a huge metal building,
mouth wide open with two grinding machines inside.

I unloaded the metal and started to the barn. I was jolted
by a loud whistle. I stopped, screeching the tires. "You're
driving through the parking lot. I said to hug the fence.
You want to start this all over again?" "No Mam.'"

I made it into the barn and started unloading.
Her absence surprised me until I was about to throw
a Christmas snow globe into the pile mildly concerned
if it had chemicals in it. She appeared from nowhere.

"If you offer that to me and ask me if I would
like to have it, I can take that." I did. "I used
to have a snow globe collection to beat all, then
I stored it in the attic one winter. Snow globe is
water. Everyone of 'em exploded. Every last one."

I saw her eyes tear up as she held the globe. She turned it over
and back and watched the glitter snow down on Rudolf and
the Dentist and the Abominable Snowman and Cornelius.

I hugged her without thought.

"Go on, git, and hug the fence on the way out; I need a cigarette."

Estate Sale

My wife and I have an agreement that if I'm about
to do something and she needs alone time, she
has the right to suggest I leave a bit early. I understand.

I decided to kick around close to where we were rehearsing.
I stumbled on an estate sale. I've seen all that pickin' pawn
shop shit, so I thought I might go try my hand at the real thing.

Just before the house I was already uneasy; the lawn
was green, not neglected. The water hose rolled up
meticulously, the two ends screwed into itself, a snake
eating it's own tail. It had a price tag on it—*a garden hose*.

A family could *not* come, clean, keep, reminisce, care?
He obviously had kept the lawn and flower beds.

Disgusted I almost turned around, but I passed the cash
machine and checkout without making eye contact. Next,
a guy stopped and asked me to empty my pockets.
He said he would do the same when I left. Just precaution.

I rabbit-eared my jeans. Just inside, there were rocks,
museum display items, geodes, almost a spelunker cave
of a geologist in the front room; he even constructed a
section center of the house, probably based on some Stonehenge,
with an open roof and a rather intimidating telescope pointed

toward some distant galaxy. He had done inside his house, the things
we all do in our own brain, but no one ever gets to see. A room
of mirrors, cameras, glass lenses too intricate to even explore.

"You missed the turquoise. One guy got 3,288.00 worth market-
weight alone. He stuck out his tongue and made a face like a time-
share salesman. For the second time I almost left.

The bathroom was half empty soap bottles, essentials, a pull bar
low enough so someone alone could pull themselves up. In the

bedroom next to it was just the bed and a phone bed level.
Now my fifth grade Encyclopedia Brown kicked in. He
must have been older and probably ill.

In the garage a young man was reordering things.
"Some sonofabitch stole the Dremel out of the box."
Must have put it in a boot or something.
He shook his head. "Who would steal from the dead?"

The garage looked as if rats had eaten
only the meat, leaving the bones. I turned left to

one last room. I had found his study. I held a
portable planetarium. I tried to start an old hand
held 35 millimeter camera, probably no one else
had even tried. I crossed to the other side of his work
desk. Where he sat. Books: planetary, geology, aviation
Then, I looked to the floor, the journal on the top read,
"Beating Prostrate Cancer." I've never felt sick, laughed,
and cried before all at once. I decided I wasn't much of a collector.

I started out and noticed the family Bible. People keep
real things in family bibles for some reason. My first
shock was to find his obituary in the first few pages
along with a yellowed wedding article from 1952,
his life flattened to a black-and-white clipping two
weeks old. I looked at the photo, and imagined him
young, his whole life's work ahead of him, passionate,
like a new employee cleaning out an old office, smiling,
placing all his new treasures carefully in their places,
a shrine, just knowing what grand fight
the family would eventually have over it all.

The Minotaur

Daedalus constructed a wooden cow, hollowed out the inside completely, covered the outside with cowhide, and placed it, with wheels under its hoofs, in the meadow where the bull usually grazed. Daedalus then helped Pasiphae hide inside. The bull appeared in the meadow, mounted the decoy and impregnated Pasiphae. In time, Pasiphae gave birth to a monster that had a bull's head and a human body. Its name was Asterius, but it became known as the Minotaur.

—BULFINCH

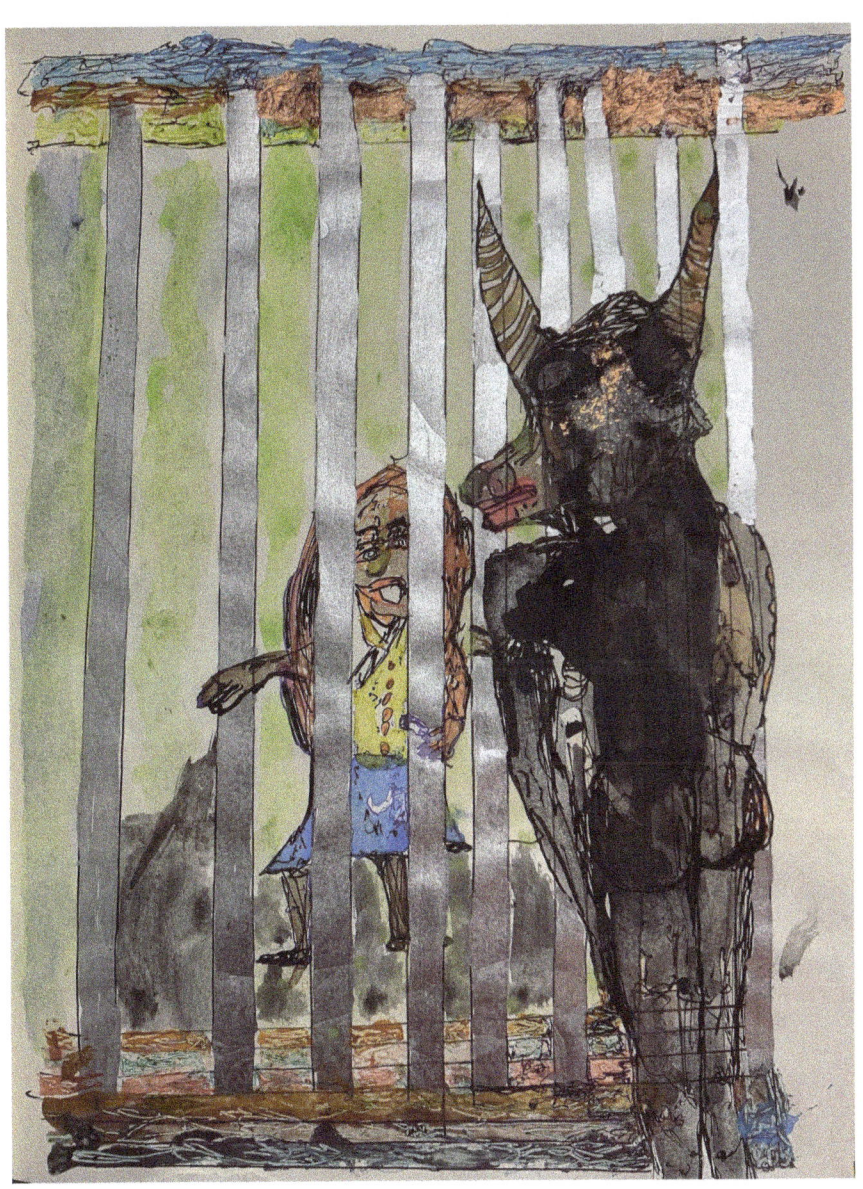

He looked ridiculous in the cage. He was a bull,
no doubt, with strong horns and muzzle, eyes black,
taut skin. But below the head of the bull
was a human torso, strong but a bit dwarfed
by the large head; nevertheless, it was not
a body to scoff at. He seemed more human than animal,
but still a bit detached. Even so, he would
have looked even more strange reversed: a human
head on the wild body of a bull; his tone
was the difference between the tame muscles of a domesticated
dog and those of a coyote caught in bright lights
drinking water at midnight from a playa lake:
stark, harsh, powerful, wild and mysterious.

The circus workers discovered him in a cave
in Italy after a show and decided he was exotic enough to keep,
even though he didn't do anything.
They chased him for miles; very difficult to catch,
very intelligent, and seemed familiar with the territory.
They finally played several men against him
in a box canyon until he was backed into an exact
corner. Even then he seemed very conniving, very thoughtful.
After they caged him, the circus didn't pay
him much attention. He was rather average;
again didn't do anything; still
he was interesting enough to look at
for the path that led to the actual circus tent: an oddity.

The circus was the last of the "Big Tops"
the advertisement read The World's Greatest Big Top;
it probably was not, but still it was billed that way.
The last circus through the small town circuit
sported a woman contortionist center stage
who pulled her body like a rubber band into
rubbery conditions. The women were amazed
and the men were disturbed by her agility
and they pictured her in erotic positions
and made side comments, "Wish my wife
could do that in bed," between hot dog bites
and sips of Coke laced with whiskey.

But again, the Minotaur didn't do anything.
He was an attraction merely because he was strange
to look at-- ridiculous. He stood rather staunch,
almost as if in contemplation rather
than in ignorance when passersby stopped
to look at him. He never 'spoke' except
to moo; a kind of a glottal, domesticated
declaration, but seldom with any regularity.

The gatekeeper had taken the cover off the cage
early that morning and the curious crowd from
town had already started to mill back
and forth on the highway in front of the circus. Some
of the circus was still in transit from the previous town,
so the grounds lay in a great maze of trucks
and trailers and cages. The gatekeeper, because
of the clean sunshine, had taken the cover
off of the Minotaur's cage and the Minotaur was left
standing hands folded in front of his body,
with his strong calves against the bale of hay
in the center of the cage. The gatekeeper
originally put the bale of hay in the cell
for the Minotaur to eat, but the Minotaur chose
merely to stand in front of it using it only
as a reference point to the other dimensions in the cage;
he moved out of instinct more than by eyesight

the gatekeeper had noticed; the Minotaur seemed
to be more comfortable in the dark.

The gatekeeper cleaned the cage as always, using
a long stick to pull the flooring hay
and dung out through a hatch; he still didn't trust
the Minotaur enough to enter the cage, even though
the Minotaur had never given any reason for alarm.

It was about an hour later, after the new
floor of soil and hay had been set, that
the first scattering of curious people began
to arrive. The gatekeeper made sure the concessions

were open before he took his usual seat
beside the cage. The first to stop were
a father and his daughter. "Look honey.
See the animal?" The man pointed then looked
to the gatekeeper for an explanation, but
the gatekeeper merely turned, as Carnies do,
away from the patrons; this was his time to rest.
"What is he?"
                      The gatekeeper hesitantly responded,
"He's an oddity. Six feet sir," he added
as he pushed the man on the hip with his long
stick used to clean the cage. "Six feet,"
he repeated with the indifference of a lion
tamer who had just put his head into
the lion's mouth yet again as he pointed
to the sign with a stick. It was almost
as if he were protecting the privacy of a side-show
fat lady rather than a dangerous oddity.

"Is he in the show? What does he do?"
 the father asked.
              "What do you want mister? For him to perform
  on the trapeze?"
                  "Does he? That's great!"

The gatekeeper picked popcorn shells from his teeth
and continued slowly and deliberately, "He's doing
what he does. He stands there. That's all."

"That's all? This is it?"
        "He's just
strange. Isn't that enough?"
              "I suppose."

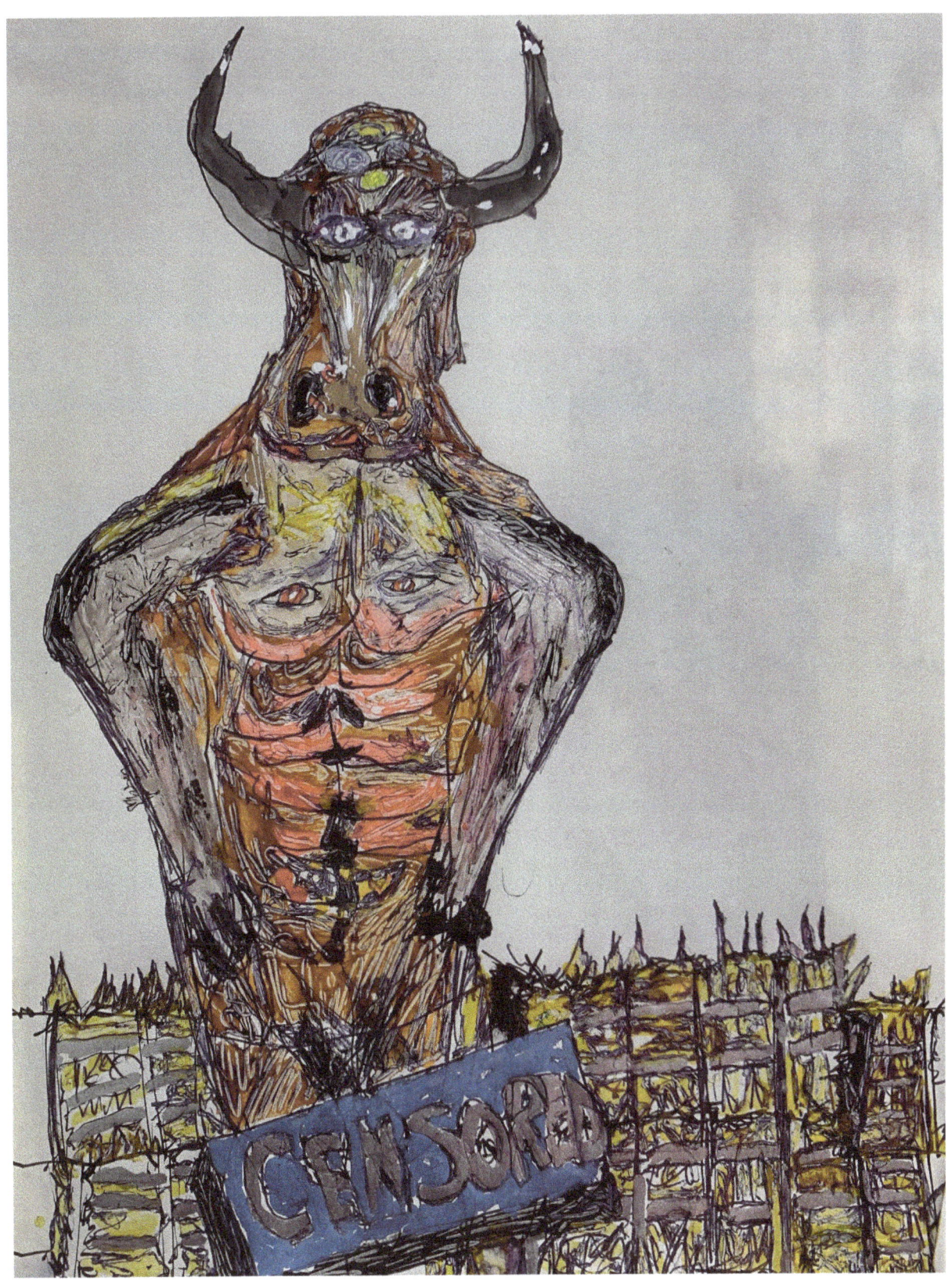

"He mooed at me." Suddenly the little girl spoke up.
"Well, move back. Give him
some space." The father moved the girl back
by grabbing her chest and back and guided her
away from the cage.
"Moooo." She *mooed* back
at the Minotaur.
"Moooo." The Minotaur *mooed* back.
The father took the girl's hand and tugged
her a bit. As the girl reluctantly turned to leave,
the Minotaur grabbed the rails and shook them with
his strong fists until the girl turned back
around; then, he calmly backed up and returned
to his position standing in the center of the hay-filled cage.

"He sleeps standing up," the guard started.
"Now, *that's* something to see. But he's so
sporadic as to when he's gonna do it
that we can't bill him in the show."

"Mooo." The girl resumed her mooing.
"Honey,
I'll run and get the tickets and some snacks.
You stay here." The girl acknowledged her father's
leaving with a head nod while
at the same time beginning a new *moo*.

The girl and the Minotaur were *mooing* when more
people began to stop.
"What's this?" a new father asked
"The Minotaur," a Mexican father answered
like a person who knew. "Course it's not real.
You can see where they sewed the head
on him. But it's still a good job. The guy's
doin' a damn good job."
The gatekeeper started
to say something but then merely shifted
in his chair and then said, "Six feet.
That's the closest."
"What does he do?" the new

88

father asked the Mexican.
                              "He moos," the little girl
interrupted. She *mooed* to demonstrate and the Minotaur
mooed. The people responded by trying their *moos*.
He responded sporadically to some, but always to
the little girl, so she became the official, "One-who-
could-make-the-Minotaur-*moo*" when new
observers joined the group she was always
encouraged by the group to prove it.

The Minotaur started to reach behind with his hand.
The gatekeeper hit the cage with his stick
and the Minotaur straightened back up.

"No! No!" The gatekeeper was obviously reprimanding
the Minotaur, but it was not evident why.

"What's the discipline for?" one father asked.
"Sometimes he throws his dung."
                              "That's gross,"
the girl said.
              "I've seen gorillas do
that in the zoo," the Mexican added.
The Minotaur *mooed* again.
                              "He sounds real."
"And he sleeps standing up," another man
 said to a newcomer.
                  "Well, horses sleep
standing up. That's no big deal,"
                              the Mexican said.

"Still, he's half-man, half-animal."
Who ain't," the Mexican father
poked the other man in the ribs.
                              "Does he
like these? What'll he do with a peanut?"
A farmer with a heavy West Texas accent threw
a peanut in the cage and it hit the bale
of hay beside the Minotaur and bounced back
and sat at the Minotaur's feet. The Minotaur bent

89

and picked the peanut up, cracked it in
his teeth and ate it and then placed his hands
back together in front of his body.
"Just like a damn monkey."
                        "Let me throw
one daddy."
            "Don't feed the animal," the keeper
said, but not with much conviction.
                        "C'mon,
who're you kidding? He's not an animal. He's
a human with a bull mask," the Mexican father
responded.
              "Dad. C'mon let me throw one."
"Here." He gave the boy a fist full
of peanuts. The boy threw the peanuts one
at a time and watched the Minotaur crouch
to get each one and eat it. After a while
the boy threw the peanuts, one at a time,
far into the corners and behind the Minotaur.
While the Minotaur was crouched to get one
the boy threw another, but the Minotaur
methodically picked up each one, even
those behind him that he couldn't have known
were even thrown. The boy gave a few
peanuts to his smaller brother. The two
boys scattered the pen again with nuts,
and once again the Minotaur selected each one,
leaving none, picking off the floor—in order.

"See if he likes corndogs."
                    "People! Look,
don't feed the animal, not the corndog,"
the gatekeeper responded with a bit more
conviction this time.

The pinched off piece of corndog hit the Minotaur
in the muzzle and fell to the hay
and then to the floor. The Minotaur didn't
move. The younger boy threw another

piece slightly bigger and hit the Minotaur
in the chest; it glanced off leaving
a smudge of ketchup just below his throat
on the left side of his chest.
      "Hit 'em
in the nose again."
    "He'll just stand there."

In a matter of minutes everyone was trying any
type of food possible: peanuts, rolled
balls of cotton candy, pieces of ice, popcorn.

Suddenly the Minotaur seemed to wake from years
of domestication. And as if tearing
through years of sublimation, he became
a monstrous messenger of his mother's perverted
passion. He rushed the bars and took them
in his hands. Luckily the cage was well-made,
too twentieth-century to budge under
the mere hands of an ancient beast; still,
the metal rang out across the circus yard.
The crowd pulled back quickly but didn't run.
Instead, they viewed it like a horror movie
that was taking place safely on screen,
or inside a TV tube, or stage with
the Phantom safe inside the proscenium wall.
"Arrrrrghhhh!" The Mexican father growled back
at the Minotaur much like one
does to wild dogs who are safely caged.
    "It's all part of the show," he explained
to those around him. "He don't do
anything, huh?" He threw an aside to
the keeper who now was sincerely concerned
with the animal. But the Minotaur didn't settle;
it was as if he were finding years of bestial
passion rushing forward through time
and overwhelming him. His docile *moo*
twisted into an animal shriek, a cry
almost like that of a bull trapped

with a small rider in a small chute, bull
and rider the same, unable to throw himself off.

Even during the shaking and bellowing, the crowd,
who had been mildly alarmed at first, quickly
lost their fear and began to tighten the space
between people as more and more poured
onto their backs. As the crowd grew tighter,
though larger with each passing moment, they forced
the little girl forward and encouraged her
to magically *moo* at the beast. Instead though,
the girl pointed at him and imitated
his shriek rather than his *moo*.

Without any warning, the Minotaur suddenly
reached across time, and in a second
he had the girl against the bars, trying
to pull and force her body through the bars.

Her eyes were wide open when her neck
popped. Even then, he didn't drop her;
instead, he held her arms' length
and flailed her limp body; then again
he pulled her stiff against the bars
with a metal ring, then held her limp
again at arms' length. Finally, he dropped
her onto the dust and packed dirt, where
she lay twisted like fresh green roots.

Without hesitation the gatekeeper fired a shotgun
blast through the bars into the Minotaur's chest.
Some pellets ricocheted off the bars and into
the crowd causing the crowd to cover their eyes.
Another shot took the Minotaur to his knees.
His animal shriek started shrill but fell
into itself, his chest caved in, his voice
returning across time, back into the darkness.
Another shot took part of his horn and mauled
his muzzle. He was probably dead before

he even hit the floor, but the keeper
in his excitement was merely making sure.

The Minotaur lay face down as a last
snort of air shot from his nostrils across
the floor of the cage stirring the hay in a small
whirlwind that sputtered and settled by his twitching
human hand which lay clutching the soil;
he was dead—finally. The father of
the child laid his body like a blanket across the girl.

The crowd began to churn and grow; none
of the newcomers were exactly sure what
had happened suspected something of great
 proportion.
    "He just suddenly went crazy,"
the gatekeeper started to explain. "Beats anything
I ever seen." In the back of the crowd a newcomer
man pushed a bit too tightly against
the back of another bystander.
       "Hey, watch it.
Leave some room, will ya?"
       "What happened?"
"Shhhhhh!" The man listened intensely as
the gatekeeper described the already altering story
of the little girl's death.
     "Slammed
her into the bar," someone added
to the gatekeeper's spiel.
      "Well, hell.
I missed the whole damn thing." the newcomer
said as he lifted himself on his toes trying
to see some clue in order to piece the whole
incident together, and he was angry and envious
as he knew he had missed something truly spectacular.

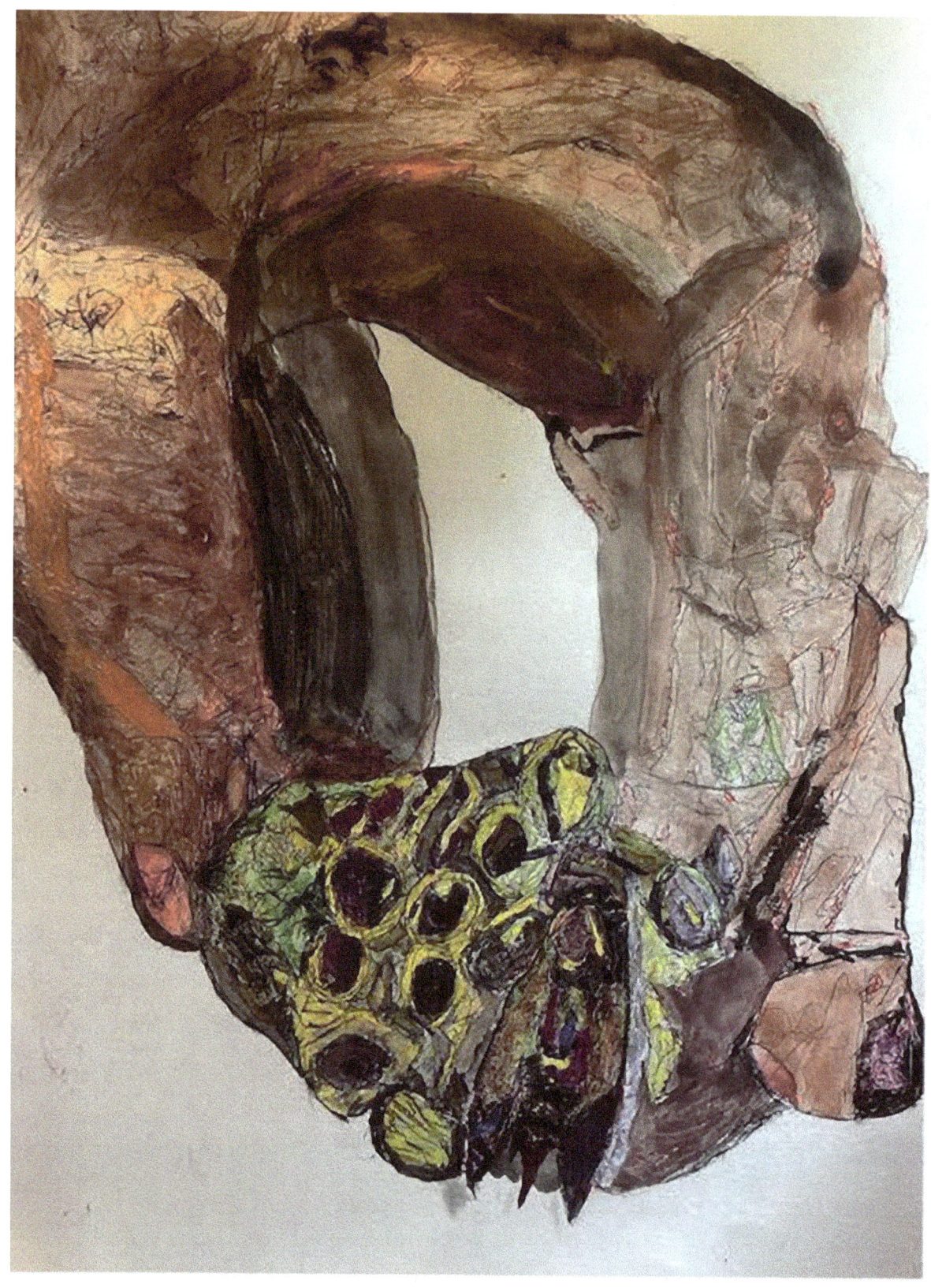

Maiden's Name Game

Please, give me your grandmother's maiden name;
then tell me where her mother's grave sits.
Say the name of your grandfather's mother the same.

Memory is short, short as a drunk man's claim.
But ants still build, and geese still never miss.
Please, give me your grandmother's maiden name;

The pod of whales just left globe's top the game
behind the door where you cannot hear their bliss.
Say the name of your grandfather's mother the same.

The whales're at your door, "Hear their name?"
swimming, blow-holes, geysers, growing hiss.
Please, Give me your grandmother's maiden name;

And there, where bodies hide, boiling blame,
blue, memory and recollect watery bliss.
Say the name of your grandfather's mother the same.

Wasps curve their baskets in attempt to tame
their children who'll forget them just the same.
Please, Give me your grandmother's maiden name;
Say the name of your grandfather's mother the same.

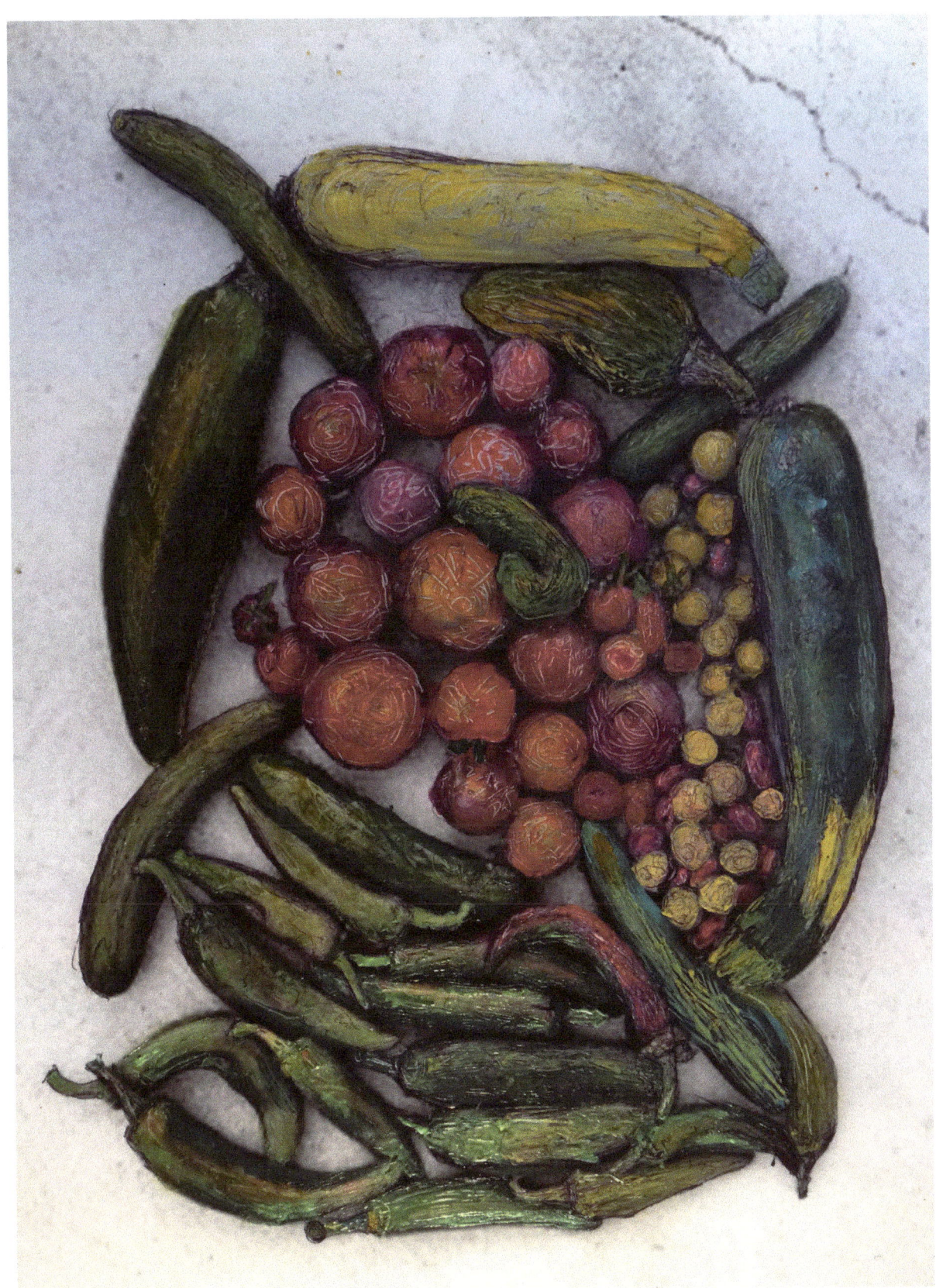